Carolyn
Dupuy

Identifying and Tearing Down Strongholds

A Journey to Wholeness

Breaking Chains That Bind ™

CAROLYN DUPUY

WESTBOW®
PRESS
A DIVISION OF THOMAS NELSON
& ZONDERVAN

New Revised Standard Version Bible, copyright 1989, Division of Christian Education of the National Council of the Churches of Christ in the United States of America. Used by permission. All rights reserved.

Scripture taken from the King James Version of the Bible.

Scriptures taken from the Holy Bible, New International Version®, NIV®. Copyright © 1973, 1978, 1984, 2011 by Biblica, Inc.™ Used by permission of Zondervan. All rights reserved worldwide. www.zondervan.com The "NIV" and "New International Version" are trademarks registered in the United States Patent and Trademark Office by Biblica, Inc.™ All rights reserved.

All Hebrew and Greek definitions are taken from Quick Verse 2011 version 15.0.21 for personal computers.

Recovery Outreach Ministry, Inc.
P.O. Box 766
Berwick, LA 70342
985-519-2671
www.recoveryoutreachministry.org
carolyn@recoveryoutreachministry.org

Rev. Carolyn Dupuy, CBT
Founder and President of Recovery Outreach Ministry, Inc.

WestBow Press books may be ordered through booksellers or by contacting:

WestBow Press
A Division of Thomas Nelson & Zondervan
1663 Liberty Drive
Bloomington, IN 47403
www.westbowpress.com
1 (866) 928-1240

ISBN: 978-1-4908-2862-6 (sc)
ISBN: 978-1-4908-2860-2 (hc)
ISBN: 978-1-4908-2861-9 (e)
Library of Congress Control Number: 2014904187

Printed in the United States of America.
WestBow Press rev. date: 04/28/2014

❧ Contents ❧

Foreword...xi

Introduction...xiii

Questionnaire xv

Spirit, Soul, and Body...1

  Part 1...1

    We Are Made in God's Image 1

    Spirit 2

    Soul 3

    Body 3

    We Must Be Born Again to Enter the Kingdom of Heaven 5

    Changing Our Soul Realm 6

    Walking in the Spirit..7

      Home Study Guide 10

      Morning Prayer of Consecration...13

      Notes 14

Spiritual Laws and Cycles 16

  Part 2...16

    The Law of the Spirit of Life vs. the Law of Sin and Death.......18

    Natural Laws vs. Spiritual Laws 19

    Sir Isaac Newton's Three Laws of Motion 20

    Conception with Adamic Nature..23

    Action of an Authority Figure 24

    How to Honor Authority...28

    Anger 31

    Bitterness 36

    Forgiveness/Unforgiveness...37

Judgment...47

Inner Vow...51

Heart of Stone 55

Wounded/Slumbering Spirit.. 60

Expectations..62

Reap in Kind (Newton's Third Law of Motion).......... 66

Journey to Wholeness 67

    Home Study Guide 70

    Morning Prayer of Consecration........................ 80

    Prayers for Deliverance...81

    Notes...86

Healing Gestational Wounds... 88

  Part 3.. 88

  A Baby in the Womb Aware of His Surroundings.....................89

  Jewish Culture 90

  Jacob and Esau... 90

  Predestined before the Foundation of the World...................91

  Experiences of the Unborn 92

  Conditions That Can Affect the Unborn Child..........92

  Solution 94

    Home Study Guide 95

    Prayer for Deliverance 96

    Notes...97

Soul Ties 99

  Part 4.. 99

  Spirit 99

  Soul 99

  Body 100

  Godly Soul Ties..100

  Parent-and-Child Soul Ties 101

  Generational Curses/Soul Ties..................................102

  Perfect Soul Tie: Marriage...102

  Destructive Sexual Soul Ties 104

  Do Not Withhold Sex from Your Spouse 106

Divorce and Sexual Soul Ties 107

Destructive Controlling Soul Ties 108

Unforgiveness...108

Relationships 109

Three Levels of Soul Ties 110

How to Get Free 111

How to Renew the Mind 111

    Home Study Guide 112

    Prayer for Deliverance 114

    Notes..115

Generational Curses I...117

  Part 5...117

    Origination of Curses 117

    God's Covenant of Blessings with Abraham 118

    God's Covenant with Abraham Applies to Us Today 119

    Abraham's Blessings Continue.....................................120

    Curses 120

    Christ Delivered Us from the Curse 121

    A Baby Born into This World Is Not Born Again 122

    We Must Take by Force What Belongs to Us 122

    God Gives Us a Choice...122

    Curses Have Causes 123

    Curses upon Our Seed 124

    Manifestations of Curses 125

    Ways We Perpetuate Generational Curses....................126

    Notes..127

Generational Curses II 128

  Part 6...128

    Ignorance of Curses...129

    Sources of Curses 129

    The Breaking of God's Laws Is Sin...............................130

    Open Doors for Curses...133

    Purposes of Curses 134

    Generational Curse, Abraham to Isaac.........................137

Involvement with Unclean and Unholy Things 141
Examples of Mythological Gods 146
How to Break Curses 148
   Conclusion 150
   Home Study Guide 152
   Prayer for Deliverance 154
   Notes 155
   Illustrations 161

Bibliography 163
About the Author 165

This study guide is dedicated to my beloved husband, companion, and friend of twenty-six years for all the patience and love he has shown while God was working His miracles in our lives. Sometimes I did not know if we would make it through the journey, but I am so glad we did. It has been well worth it!

This book is also dedicated to all those along the way who have helped me become the woman of God I am today and to all those who participate in this study, seeking God for answers to their persistent problems.

But above all this work is dedicated to my Daddy God for the mercy and the grace He has offered me along the way. He looked beyond what I was to what I could become with His help.

Thank you, Daddy God; I love you with my life!

❧ *Foreword* ❦

Have you ever wondered what life would look like if you were free?

All your addictions would be gone, all your pain confronted. Your past would be redeemed. Your present would make sense. Your future would be secure. One of the greatest joys in my life is walking in the freedom that Christ has provided for me through His life, death, and resurrection. Unfortunately, it has been my experience that many people who have accepted Christ as their Savior are not living in the freedom He has provided.

That's why *Identifying and Tearing Down Strongholds* is such an important book.

Carolyn Dupuy and her husband, Merrill, have been faithful members of our church for several years. They have been involved in church for the better part of their lives. Both have servant's hearts, and I can say with all certainty that Carolyn's teaching is biblically based and solid. I believe with all my heart that she communicates the truth of the gospel with love. That is truly transformational.

Carolyn is personally responsible for the recovery of many people in our church. I have watched as the principles she uses promote health in individuals who had struggled with many different forms of addictive behavior and personality disorders. She also handles the majority of the counseling load for our church. I have never seen her refuse to meet with anyone, and if people commit to the process she has created almost all see tremendous results.

This process works. It's not a quick fix. But it is a journey toward wholeness. If you choose to engage in this process, you can be everything God has created you to be. And I've learned this: the secret to a rich and satisfying life is found when you reconnect with the purpose God planned for you. That happens as you walk in the freedom Christ has provided for you. It's the next step after trusting Him as your personal Savior. This book will teach you how to make Him Lord over every area of your life.

It is a privilege for me to write these words to you. I can tell you that you are on the edge of the most incredible journey of your life. Please take that next step. I promise that freedom is waiting!

Den Hussey

Campus Pastor

The Crossing Place Fellowship

Morgan City, LA 70380

❧ Introduction ❧

In her book *Shattering Your Strongholds,* Christian author Liberty S. Savard writes, "A stronghold is what one uses to fortify and defend a personal belief, idea or opinion against outside opposition. A stronghold is the fortification around and defense of what you believe, especially when you are dead wrong."

In this study, I will examine spiritual laws regarding strongholds. My goal is to teach you to recognize these principles found in the Word of God and to see how they affect your life for better or for worse. With the help of the Holy Spirit, I will also teach you how to destroy these strongholds, creating the atmosphere for the Holy Spirit to take you into a deeper relationship not only with Himself, but with God our Father.

This study will require determination, perseverance, and self-sacrifice on your part. You will have to seek God to find answers to your issues. I hope to provide you with the tools for this journey.

Get ready, tighten your spiritual seat belt, set your expectancies on high alert, and let us delve into the Word of God together.

"That the God of our Lord Jesus Christ, the Father of glory, may give unto you the spirit of wisdom and revelation in the knowledge of him: The eyes of your understanding being enlightened; that ye may know what is the hope of his calling, and what the riches of the glory of his inheritance in the saints" (Ephesians 1:17–18 KJV).

Knowledge is power, and the application
of that knowledge is wisdom.

❧ *Questionnaire* ❦

Take a few minutes to read the questions below, then journal your thoughts regarding anything that comes to mind. Your responses to these questions may surprise you and make you aware of issues concealed deep within your subconscious. Be as truthful as you can. There are no right or wrong answers to these questions. Their sole purpose is to help you become more aware of buried issues that you may not have processed in a godly manner.

1.) Do you often get offended?
2.) Do you rehash past pain with friends/relatives?
3.) Has someone hurt you so much that you have said, "I can't forgive him/her for what he/she did to me"?
4.) Do you want to forgive someone but find that the memory of past pain still affects you today?
5.) Do you overreact when someone does something to hurt you? Do you brood over or rehash the pain for days or even years?
6.) Are you filled with anger, bitterness, or resentment toward someone who hurt you in the past?
7.) Do you hide painful emotions instead of confronting them with love?
8.) Do you blame everyone else for the troubles or failures in your life?
9.) Do you say, "I'm just the way I am because of the family I came from"? Or "All of my relatives act this way, so I guess I'll be this way forever"?
10.) Are you aware of hidden vows you have made to keep someone from hurting you again?

11.) Are you having trouble sustaining relationships? Have you had multiple divorces or gone from church to church or relationship to relationship? Do you withdraw from relationships because of a fear of being offended or rejected?

12.) Do you have problems that you cannot seem to overcome?

13.) Do you abhor certain characteristics about yourself, but find yourself unable to control or to change them?

14.) Can you remember and recount painful memories without getting emotional and reliving the pain?

15.) As a child, were you emotionally, verbally, physically, or sexually abused?

16.) Do you have trouble setting boundaries because you are afraid of rejection?

17.) Do you stay in an abusive relationship out of fear of being alone?

If you answered yes to any of these questions, you may have a problem hidden deep within your soul realm. You may have hidden unforgiveness, judgments, rejection, abandonment issues, betrayal, unmet needs, damaged emotions, or other issues in your subconcious and may not realize that they exist.

Your relationship with Jesus, the Holy Spirit, and our heavenly Father is a journey that will take a lifetime. You will not become perfect, not while you are in the flesh and dwell on earth, so do not be discouraged if you suffer from dysfunction or character flaws. You must press on in the Spirit and become all you can be in Christ one day at a time.

Let's open the Word of God and see what our heavenly Father has to say concerning the roots of our problems and the godly way to resolve them.

_____

_____

_____

_____

_____

_____

_____

_____

_____

_____

_____

_____

_____

_____

_____

_____

_____

_____

_____

_____

_____

_____

_____

_____

_____

_____

_____

_____

_____

_____

_____

_____

_____

_____

Spirit, Soul, and Body

Part 1

We Are Made in God's Image

> And God said, "Let us make man in our image, after our likeness: and let them have dominion over the fish of the sea, and over the fowl of the air, and over the cattle, and over all the earth, and over every creeping thing that creepeth upon the earth." So God created man in his own image, in the image of God created he him; male and female created he them.
>
> —Genesis 1:26–27 KJV

The Godhead is triune, consisting of three persons in one, the Father, the Son, and the Holy Ghost. Therefore, when God said, "Let us make man in our image," He implied that He would create all humanity in the same manner. All human beings would be fashioned with three parts—a spirit, a soul, and a body. As a result, we are spirits, we have souls, and we live in bodies.

Satan used a threefold appeal to deceive Adam and Eve. First was a lust of the flesh, a physical approach that appealed to their bodies; second was a lust of the eye, which appealed to their thinking or

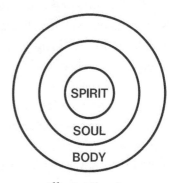

Illustration 1 –
Spirit, Soul & Body

1

emotions; third was a pride of life, a spirit that appealed to the core of their beings. He continues to employ this strategy with us.

"And the very God of peace sanctify you wholly; and I pray God your whole spirit and soul and body be preserved blameless unto the coming of our Lord Jesus Christ" (1 Thessalonians 5:23 KJV).

Spirit

Pneuma is the God consciousness that allows communication with the Almighty; it is the part of us that knows. The Spirit's agenda is to be holy, to pursue holiness or rightness with God.

"For what man knoweth the things of a man, save the spirit of man which is in him? even so the things of God knoweth no man, but the Spirit of God" (1 Corinthians 2:11 KJV).

"But there is a spirit in man: and the inspiration of the Almighty giveth them understanding" (Job 32:8 KJV).

"For the word of God is quick, and powerful, and sharper than any two-edged sword, piercing even to the dividing asunder of soul and spirit, and of the joints and marrow, and is a discerner of the thoughts and intents of the heart" (Hebrews 4:12 KJV).

God is the only one who can know what is hidden in the depths of our souls and our spirits. He alone is capable of seeing the contents of our spirits, shining His light on the areas that are not pleasing to Him. He alone is capable of leading us to wholeness.

We will never achieve wholeness without the help of the Holy Spirit. When we look at one another, we see only the bodies that house our souls and our spirits. No one can see the reality of who we are deep within our spirits unless God makes that known.

Soul

The psyche is self-consciousness, mind, will, intellect, emotions, desires, imagination, conscience, memory, reason, affections, curiosity, perception, and desires. The soul's agenda is to be happy and at peace with God (Philippians 4). "Why art thou cast down, O my soul? And why art thou disquieted in me? Hope thou in God: for I shall yet praise him for the help of His countenance. O my God, my soul is cast down within me: therefore will I remember thee from the land of Jordan, and of the Hermonites, from the hill Miza" (Psalm 42:5–6 KJV).

In this passage, David spoke of his soul, or his mind, will, emotions, and intellect, being in a state of depression, anxiety, uneasiness, restlessness, and dissatisfaction. As he recognized and declared his mental state to God, he remembered where his help came from and confessed that it was from God alone. "The heart *is* deceitful above all *things*, and desperately wicked: who can know it? I the LORD search the heart, *I* try the reins, even to give every man according to his ways, *and* according to the fruit of his doings." (Jeremiah 17:9–10 KJV).

The word *heart* in this verse is *labe* in the original Hebrew, meaning "the soul." The word *deceitful* is *aqob* in the Hebrew, which can be translated as a knoll, or something swelling up because it is crooked or polluted.

Body

The *soma* is the seat of the senses—sight, hearing, smell, taste, and touch—the means by which the spirit and the soul have world consciousness, and the locus of man's fallen Adamic nature. The body's agenda is to be healthy, safe, comfortable, and physically satisfied. "And the Lord God formed man of the dust of the ground, and breathed into his nostrils the breath of life; and man became a living soul" (Genesis 2:7 KJV).

After God formed him from the dust of the earth, Adam lay on the ground—an object just like any other lifeless form without the breath of God. When God breathed into his nostrils, Adam took into himself the spirit of God, the giver of all life, and became a living soul. By breathing into Adam, God imparted into him a soul and a spirit that would live eternally.

We all choose where we will spend eternity—whether in heaven or in hell. Our destinies are a result of obedience or disobedience to God and His Word. God gives to all His creation the freedom of choice. We choose whether we will serve God in obedience or reject His Son. If we choose obedience to God, we will spend eternity with Him; if we choose disobedience, we will spend eternity in hell. There is no in between; either we love and serve Him or we reject Him. "And unto the angel of the church of the Laodiceans write; These things saith the Amen, the faithful and true witness, the beginning of the creation of God; I know thy works, that thou art neither cold nor hot: I would thou wert cold or hot. So then because thou art lukewarm, and neither cold nor hot, I will spue thee out of my mouth" (Revelation 3:14–16 KJV).

The word *spue* in the original Hebrew is *emeo*, meaning "to vomit." (Quick Verse Essentials 2011 for personal computers)

The body is separate from the spirit and the soul and therefore subject to physical death. "And just as we have borne the image of the earthy, we shall also bear the image of the heavenly. Now I say this, brethren, that flesh and blood cannot inherit the kingdom of God; nor does the perishable inherit the imperishable" (1 Corinthians 15:49–50 NASB).

"What? know ye not that your body is the temple of the Holy Ghost which is in you, which ye have of God, and ye are not your own? For ye are bought with a price: therefore glorify God in your body, and in your spirit, which are God's" (1 Corinthians 6:19 KJV).

God expects us to treat our bodies like the temples of God that they are. "And thou shalt love the Lord thy God with all thy heart, and with all thy soul, and with all thy mind, and with all thy strength: this is the first commandment. And the second is like, namely this, Thou shalt love thy neighbour as thyself. There is none other commandment greater than these" (Mark 12:30–31).

Our earthly flesh will never inherit eternal life. With the help of the Holy Spirit, we must keep the body under submission, because it is impossible to sanctify the flesh. Given the right circumstances, our flesh will always revert to its old, sinful ways. Residing deep within the flesh is the propensity to be self-centered and react according to the sinful nature residing within.

"Nay, in all these things we are more than conquerors through him that loved us" (Romans 8:37 KJV). We are more than conquerors by daily feasting on the Word of God and keeping fellowship with our holy Father.

We Must Be Born Again to Enter the Kingdom of Heaven

> Jesus answered and said unto him, Verily, verily, I say unto thee, Except a man be born again, he cannot see the kingdom of God ... Jesus answered, Verily, verily, I say unto thee, Except a man be born of water and of the Spirit, he cannot enter into the kingdom of God.
>
> —John 3:3, 5

We are born once into this world by water through natural birth to our mothers. This is what Jesus was speaking about in John 3:5. We must be born again in our spirits to become children of God. This rebirth changes our spiritual selves, not our soul realms or our fleshly nature. If we are bad cooks, mechanics, mothers, or fathers before we experience the new birth, we will still be bad cooks, mechanics, mothers, or fathers after we are reborn.

When Adam was in the garden, he was perfect in every way—spirit, soul, and body. He communicated with God face to face. There was no separation between them, because sin had not entered into the world. Adam's disobedience to God's instruction not to eat of the Tree of Knowledge of Good and Evil created the separation between God and humanity.

This sin introduced death to the natural person and to the spiritual self, creating the need for a rebirth of the spirit and a restoration of fellowship between God and humanity. God had warned Adam of the consequences if he ate of the forbidden tree. "And the Lord God commanded the man, 'You may freely eat of every tree of the garden; but of the tree of the knowledge of good and evil you shall not eat, for in the day that you eat of it you shall die'" (Genesis 2:16–17).

Changing Our Soul Realm

And be not conformed to this world: but be ye transformed by the renewing of your mind, that ye may prove what is that good, and acceptable, and perfect, will of God.

—Romans 12:2 KJV

The apostle Paul is telling us not to conform to those unsaved persons around us. Nor are we to conform to carnal Christians who walk according to their emotions or fleshly appetites. To conform means to be in harmony with prevailing standards or customs.

Paul says we must transform ourselves by renewing our minds. The only way to do this is through the Word of God. We must begin to take on the character and the personality of Christ the Redeemer after our conversion.

The word *transformed* in the original Hebrew is *metamorphoo*. This is the same word used to describe the transformation of the caterpillar into a butterfly. The larva weaves a chrysalis around itself by excreting a stream of liquid from glands below its mouth. This liquid hardens into a silky thread that it attaches to a twig or a leaf. With this thread, it spins a shell-like covering around its body. Inside the shell, it changes into a pupa, or the body of a butterfly. This stage of development takes anywhere from ten days to several months. When it emerges, the creature is a beautiful butterfly with no resemblance to his former caterpillar state.

We are born again in the spirit when we repent and turn our lives over to Christ, but this is only the beginning of our journey toward wholeness. Our souls remain unchanged until we renew them by the Word. The only way to be clean and whole is to study and obey the Word.

As we begin this journey with Jesus, we are just like the larva, young and helpless. We are vulnerable and ignorant of Satan's wiles. As we study the Word of God, diligently applying it to our daily lives, we create a wall of protection around ourselves just as the larva creates one around itself. The Word of God covers and protects us as we speak the promises of God daily over our lives. While we are in the Word, praying and moving in His presence, we change into His image.

"But we all, with open face beholding as in a glass the glory of the Lord, are changed into the same image from glory to glory, even as by the Spirit of the Lord." (2 Corinthians 3:18 KJV).

Just as the larva excretes the stream of liquid from beneath its mouth, we should be speaking the Word, which is the sword of the Spirit. The Word of God will wash us daily, cleansing us from hidden patterns of sin from our past and bringing us into full maturity in the image of Christ Jesus.

Walking in the Spirit

> Husbands, love your wives, even as Christ also loved the
> church, and gave himself for it; that he might sanctify and
> cleanse it with the washing of water by the Word.
> —Ephesians 5:25–26 KJV

Jesus is talking about the church, believers who have had the born-again experience with Christ. The word for *sanctify* in the original Hebrew means to make holy, to purify, or to consecrate, to render physically pure and morally blameless.

"Study to shew thyself approved unto God, a workman that needeth not to be ashamed, rightly dividing the word of truth" (2 Timothy 2:15 KJV).

We are to study the Word of God and to apply the principles found there to our everyday lives. We cannot isolate a single Scripture verse and make it mean what we want it to mean. We can interpret the Word only through the Word. We must ask who is speaking, to whom he is speaking, and in what context he is speaking.

"Wherefore lay apart all filthiness, and superfluity [abundance] of naughtiness [depravity, evil, malice, wickedness], and receive with meekness the engrafted word which is able to save your souls. But be ye doers of the word, and not hearers only, deceiving your own selves" (James 1:21–22 KJV).

Studying the Word will engraft it on our hearts, making it a part of our very being. The Word will then take root and transform us into the very image of Christ, which we want to duplicate in every thought, word, and deed. We must be so in harmony with this image that when Satan sees us he does not know the difference between us and Jesus.

All sin dwells in our souls—our minds, wills, intellects, and emotions. We have inherited in our souls the sinful fallen nature of Adam and Eve. Our souls need renewing by the Word. If we do not cry out for the Holy Spirit to cleanse and change our souls, we will forever walk in our emotions and self-will.

'This I say then, Walk in the Spirit, and ye shall not fulfill the lust of the flesh. For the flesh lusteth against the Spirit, and the Spirit against the flesh: and these are contrary the one to the other: so that ye cannot do the things that ye would" (Galatians 5:16–17 KJV).

The only way to renew our minds is to study the Word of God, allowing the Holy Spirit to change our hearts. If we were complete when we were born again, why would God tell us to study the Word?

Let us examine our hearts to see if we must apply the blood of Jesus to any character traits acquired in childhood or in our experiences as adults to gain the wholeness God intended us to have in Him.

"Search me, O God, and know my heart: try me, and know my thoughts: And see if there be any wicked way in me, and lead me in the way everlasting" (Psalm 139:23–24).

Home Study Guide

Spirit, Soul, and Body

Genesis 1:16–27; 1 Thessalonians 5:23; 1 Corinthians 2:11; Job 32:8; Hebrews 4:12; Psalms 42:5–6; Jeremiah 17:9–10; Genesis 2:7; Revelation 3:14–16; 1 Corinthians 15:49–50; 1 Corinthians 6:19; Mark 12:30.

1.) We Are Made in God's Image.

2.) In what ways has Satan confronted you with the three temptations—lust of the flesh, lust of the eye, and the pride of life? What thoughts cause you later to regret your actions?

Start a journal of your thoughts as you recall your past failures. At the end of part 1, you will find notes pages for this purpose.

In the patterns that emerge, you will discover somewhere in your past an unforgiveness, a judgment, a generational curse, or a sin that opened the door for Satan to gain access to your life. Ask God to show you how this door was opened. In "Prayers for Deliverance" in part 2, you will find prayers for processing unforgiveness, judgements, and inner vows. Place each incident you recall in the blank space pertaining to that memory and process the memory or the sin. You will find a prayer to break generational curses in part 6 under "Prayers for Deliverance." Do not forget to forgive yourself. You will find that prayer in part 2.

As you develop a better understanding of a change in spirit, soul, and body, you will begin to recognize the voice of the Holy Spirit, making you more aware of the Enemy's tactics and allowing you to become more victorious in your life. You will also begin to see the lies Satan has whispered into your ear since conception. These lies created dysfunctional behavior patterns that became strongholds. You must break the chains holding you to these behaviors.

3.) Your Must Be Born Again to Enter the Kingdom of Heaven.

4.) John 3:3–5; Genesis 2:16–17; Acts 4:12; Romans 10:9–10.

Have you acknowledged your sins, asked Jesus to forgive you, and turned your life over to Him? If not, the next paragraph will lead you in the sinner's prayer. God keeps a book called the Lamb's Book of Life in which He writes every new convert's name after he or she repeats this prayer, turning his or her life over to Him.

Prayer: Father I come to You in the name of Jesus, knowing I am a sinner. I believe that Jesus died on the cross for my sins, rising on the third day. You are the truth, the light, and the way, and there is no other.

I confess all my sins before You and ask Your forgiveness. Release me now from the power of the enemy of my soul and set me free.

I give You my wrong mind-sets, strongholds, patterns of thinking, motives, and attitudes. I give You my will and pray not my will but Yours be done. I give my life to You to use any way You wish. I receive You as my Savior, in the name of Jesus. Amen.

5.) Changing Our Soul Realm.

6.) Romans 12:2; 2 Corinthians 3:18.

> ✗ Have you allowed the Word of God to change your thinking process so you always have peace regardless of your circumstances?

- ✗ Do you pray daily and spend time in the Word of God?
- ✗ Were you aware before this study that being born again was only the beginning?

Now that you realize this truth—that we must be renewed by the washing of the water of the Word—what will you do with this information?

7.) Walking in the Spirit.

8.) Ephesians 5:25–26; 2 Timothy 2:15; James 1:21–22; Galatians 5:16–17; Psalm 139:23–24.

Walking in the Spirit requires renewal of the mind that comes only by studying the Scriptures.

The morning prayer of consecration on the next page will help you keep your soul and your spirit open daily so the Holy Spirit can speak to you and continually guide you.

I pray this prayer each morning so the Holy Spirit has access to my life. He is a gentleman and will not violate your will by barging into your life if He is not invited.

Morning Prayer of Consecration

Father, I come to You in the name of Jesus. I believe that Jesus died on the cross for my sins and that You are the truth, the light, and the way; there is no other. I believe Jesus died on the cross for my sins and rose again from the dead.

I give You my wrong mind-sets, strongholds, patterns of thinking, motives, and attitudes. I give You my will, and I pray not my will but Yours be done.

I submit myself to You, spirit, soul, and body, and give myself to You as a willing living sacrifice. Use me for Your glory any way You choose. Thy kingdom come, Thy will be done in my life.

I give up all my rebellion and independence, my pride and self-centeredness, my harboring of rejection and inferiority, and my bitterness and unforgiveness. I give up all my sin and submit myself to You.

I confess all my sins before You and ask for Your forgiveness. Release me now from the power of the enemy of my soul. Because You paid the price for my sins, I forgive myself for all the wrongs of the past, and I accept myself.

In the name of Jesus Christ, I pull down every stronghold and renounce the power of Satan in my life. By faith, I now receive my release, and I thank You, Lord, for setting me free! Amen.

Notes

Notes

Spiritual Laws and Cycles

Part 2

We are locked into patterns of response derived from perceptions of past experiences, and we choose mates who are predisposed to fulfill our bitter root judgments. By the time you have completed this study, you will have a better understanding of the meaning of these two truths given me by the Holy Spirit.

God established certain natural laws and put them into place when He created the universe. These laws remain in place whether or not we are aware of them or believe in them.

Likewise there are spiritual principles found in the Word of God that work whether or not we know about them or choose to believe them. Even if we are unaware of these laws and how they operate, adhering to them will always produce a predetermined outcome.

When we disobey God's commands found in His Word, we always reap negative results whether or not we are aware of these commands or believe in them. In Hosea 4:6 God says, "My people are destroyed for lack of knowledge."

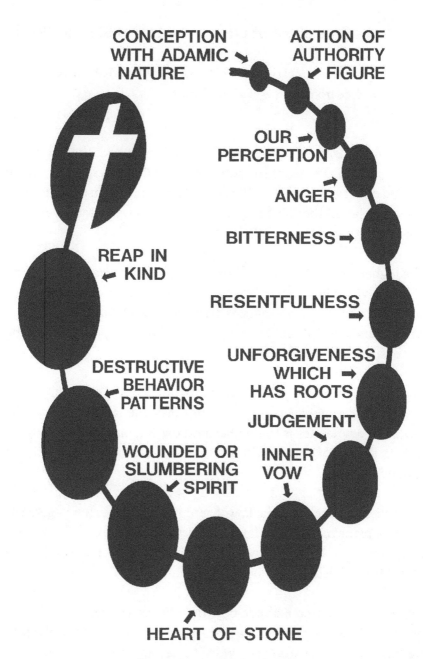

CONCEPTION WITH ADAMIC NATURE

ACTION OF AUTHORITY FIGURE

OUR PERCEPTION

ANGER

BITTERNESS

RESENTFULNESS

REAP IN KIND

UNFORGIVENESS WHICH HAS ROOTS

DESTRUCTIVE BEHAVIOR PATTERNS

JUDGEMENT

WOUNDED OR SLUMBERING SPIRIT

INNER VOW

HEART OF STONE

Illustration 2—Spiritual cycle

Knowledge is the foundation for change.

The Law of the Spirit of Life vs. the Law of Sin and Death

> For the law of the Spirit of life in Christ Jesus hath made
> me free from the law of sin and death.
> —Romans 8:2 KJV

Two major spiritual laws are operating in this world: the law of sin and death and the law of the spirit of life in Christ Jesus. The law of sin and death was at work in the fall of Adam and Eve in the garden of Eden. The law of the spirit of life in Christ Jesus was established with the crucifixion of Jesus on the cross of Calvary.

The higher law of the spirit of Christ supersedes the law of the spirit of death. When born-again believers call upon the power of the Holy Spirit and obey God's ordinances, they increase in holiness and reach a new plane of spiritual life. The power of the Spirit prevails over the law of sin and death.

The same hierarchy is at work in the natural world. For instance, the law of aerodynamics takes precedence over the law of gravity. The law of aerodynamics is the higher law, but if a plane suffers engine failure, the law of gravity will take over and the plane will fall to the ground.

Our belief or disbelief in the law of aerodynamics does not negate the fact that planes can fly. The law of gravity is another example. We may jump from a tall building, trying to disprove this law, but we will only prove its truth when we choose to defy it.

God is not a respecter of persons. He will not change His spiritual or natural laws just because we choose to remain ignorant of them. He has called us to study His Word to become informed about our inheritance and about Satan's wiles.

"Study to show thyself approved unto God, a workman that needeth not to be ashamed, rightly dividing the word of truth" (2 Timothy 2:15 KJV).

"I beseech you therefore, brethren, by the mercies of God, that ye present your bodies a living sacrifice, holy, acceptable unto God, which is your reasonable service. And be not conformed to this world: but be ye transformed by the renewing of your mind, that ye may prove what is that good, and acceptable, and perfect, will of God" (Romans 12:1-2 KJV).

Renewing the mind is possible only by studying the Word of God. Being born again does not automatically make us perfect. The only way to grow in the spirit is to study the Word.

God's Word is the ultimate law.

Let us look at laws that parallel in the spirit as well as in the natural realm.

Natural Laws vs. Spiritual Laws

Since the beginning of time and throughout Scripture, God has used natural circumstances as illustrations to convey spiritual principles or revelations to His people. He has done this to reveal Himself to humanity or to those who had ears to hear and eyes to see. He knew this was the only way they could understand the hidden things of the Spirit. He had to relate to people in terms they could understand, with things they knew about, had experienced, or could see.

Numerous times throughout the Bible, He used examples from farming, fishing, or the culture because He knew people could relate to familiar subjects and thus gain understanding. The Bible is loaded with parables using natural circumstances to convey godly revelations and principles.

Sir Isaac Newton's Three Laws of Motion

Isaac Newton's three laws of motion can be linked to principles found in the Word of God.

Newton's first law of motion states, "An object at rest will remain at rest unless acted upon by an outside force. An object in motion continues in motion with the same speed and in the same direction unless acted upon by an outside force."

This law is often called the law of inertia. God established this law when He created the universe. All objects have a natural tendency to keep on doing what they are doing; all objects resist change in whatever state they exist. In the absence of an unbalanced force, an object will maintain its state whether moving or still.

Applying this law to our spiritual lives, we can safely say that if we continue to dwell upon life's negative circumstances, our situations will not only remain the same, but will get progressively worse. The only solution is to confess God's promises over our lives until we receive the results guaranteed us in the Word of God. Thus change requires determined, persistent action on our part. The Word of God and our response to it produce the outside force that changes our lives, causing us to turn from sin to the cross of Jesus. Newton was speaking about the laws of our natural world, but this law applies to our spiritual walk as well.

Our will and obedience aligned with God's equal change.

Positive change in our lives will not occur by chance, but will require precise, determined activity. We must turn our wills over to God and make a 180-degree turn from our sins, dedicating our lives to the Lord each day and devoting time to His Word and to prayer. We must renew our minds with God's Word daily, spending time in His presence.

Change is the result of the 'unbalanced' or outside force of God in our lives functioning in us and upon us each day.

Newton's second law of motion states, "Acceleration is produced when a force acts on a mass. The greater the mass (of the object being accelerated) the greater the amount of force needed (to accelerate the object)."

Everyone unconsciously knows this second law. Everyone knows that heavier objects require more force than lighter objects to move the same distance.

Sometimes the strongholds deep within us can be removed only with fasting and prayer. That's because these strongholds have existed for so long that they have become a part of who we are and therefore they go virtually unnoticed.

> And when they were come to the multitude, there came to him a certain man, kneeling down to him, and saying, Lord, have mercy on my son: for he is a lunatic, and sore vexed: for ofttimes he falleth into the fire, and oft into the water. And I brought him to thy disciples, and they could not cure him. Then Jesus answered and said, O faithless and perverse generation, how long shall I be with you? how long shall I suffer you? bring him hither to me. And Jesus rebuked the devil; and he departed out of him: and the child was cured from that very hour. Then came the disciples to Jesus apart, and said, Why could not we cast him out?
>
> And Jesus said unto them, Because of your unbelief [disobedience or unfaithfulness]: for verily I say unto you, If ye have faith as a grain of mustard seed, ye shall say unto this mountain, Remove hence to yonder place; and it shall remove; and nothing shall be impossible unto you. Howbeit this kind goeth not out but by prayer and fasting. (Matthew 17:14–21 KJV)

When Jesus spoke about fasting and prayer, He was not talking specifically about these practices. Rather he was telling His disciples how to walk in authority and power by using the gifts of the Spirit to overcome and to deliver. Walking in the anointing would require living lives of faith and of obedience to God. In other words, the disciples would have to fast from sin and live in total surrender to God each day.

We must daily fast from sin and live lives of total surrender to God.

The longer we walk in unrepented sins and dysfunctional behavioral patterns the greater the weight of sin becomes inside our souls and spirits and the greater the consequences for our lives. The massive buildup of sin and strongholds hiding deep within us may delay the recovery process, lengthening the time before we gain the cleansing and the wholeness we seek. We will need more time to reprogram our negative thinking in accord with the Word of God.

The intent of this study is not to discourage you in your journey to recovery, but rather to encourage you to seek God with your whole being, convinced that Jesus can and will walk with you through this process into wholeness. The Lord promised He would never leave us or forsake us.

"Let your conversation be without covetousness; and be content with such things as ye have: for He hath said, I will never leave thee, nor forsake thee. So that we may boldly say, The Lord is my helper, and I will not fear what man shall do unto me" (Hebrews 13:5–6 KJV).

"Jesus answered and said unto them, Verily I say unto you, If ye have faith, and doubt not, ye shall not only do this which is done to the fig tree, but also if ye shall say unto this mountain, Be thou removed, and be thou cast into the sea; it shall be done. And all things, whatsoever ye shall ask in prayer, believing, ye shall receive" (Matthew 21:21–22 KJV).

The word for faith in Hebrew is *pistis*, which means persuasion, conviction, reliance upon Christ, constancy in profession, assurance, belief, and fidelity.

The word for doubt in Hebrew is *diakrino,* which means to separate thoroughly, to withdraw from, or oppose; to discriminate, hesitate, contend, discern, doubt, judge, be partial, stagger, or waver.

Newton's third law of motion states, "For every action there is an equal and opposite reaction." This means that for every force there is a force equal in size but opposite in direction. Thus whenever one object pushes another object, the second object pushes back equally hard in the opposite direction.

"Be not deceived; God is not mocked: for whatsoever a man soweth, that shall he also reap. For he that soweth to his flesh shall of the flesh reap corruption; but he that soweth to the Spirit shall of the Spirit reap life everlasting" (Galatians 6:7–8 KJV).

The third law of motion also applies in the spiritual realm whether or not we recognize it. This law, found in the Word of God, guarantees that whatever we do to others will come back to us.

If we submit our lives to God, manifesting integrity, fairness, mercy, and grace, we will eventually reap the benefits of our godly actions.

Unfortunately, this law also means that as we push against Satan and sin, he will without fail push right back with equal force, trying to persuade us that God is not faithful to His word.

Do not forget that sin is progressive.

Conception with Adamic Nature

Humanity has been conceived with an Adamic nature since the fall of Adam and Eve in the garden of Eden. This nature resulted from their disobedience to God's command.

"And the Lord God commanded the man, saying, Of every tree of the Garden Thou mayest freely eat: But of the tree of the knowledge of good and evil, thou shalt not eat of it: for in the day that thou eatest thereof thou shalt surely die" (Genesis 2:16–17 KJV).

"And when the woman saw that the tree was good for food, and that it was pleasant to the eyes, and a tree to be desired to make one wise, she took of the fruit thereof, and did eat, and gave also unto her husband with her; and he did eat And the eyes of them both were opened, and they knew that they were naked; and they sewed fig leaves together, and made themselves aprons" (Genesis 3:6–7 KJV).

All of us have been conceived with an Adamic nature, meaning that we have a propensity to do wrong instead of right in any given situation.

When Adam and Eve chose to partake of the fruit that Satan enticed them to eat, they became disobedient to God. As a result, sin entered the world. Since the fall of Adam and Eve in the garden of Eden, every human being has been born with a sinful nature.

Due to their sin of disobedience, God cursed the earth and everything in it. He told Eve she would give birth to her children in sorrow and told Adam he would have to toil to bring food from the ground.

Action of an Authority Figure

> Honour thy father and thy mother, as the Lord thy God
> hath commanded thee; that thy days may be prolonged,
> and that it may go well with thee, in the land which the
> Lord thy God giveth thee.
>
> —Deuteronomy 5:16

Honoring our parents means speaking well of them and addressing them politely. It also means acting in a way that shows them courtesy and respect. However, we are not to follow them in acts of disobedience to God. Parents have a special place in God's sight. Even if we find it difficult to get along with our parents, we are still required to honor them. We are to obey them until we are no longer under their care, but the responsibility to honor them continues for a lifetime.

If we do not honor our father, our mother, or other authority figures, our lives will not go well in the areas where we have disobeyed or rebelled, have had dishonor in our hearts, or have acted dishonorably toward them.

"For God commanded, saying, Honour thy father and mother: and, He that curseth father or mother, let him die the death" (Matthew 15:4).

"Whoso curseth his father or his mother, his lamp shall be put out in obscure darkness" (Proverbs 20:20).

"For Moses said, Honour thy father and thy mother; and, Whoso curseth father or mother, let him die the death" (Mark 7:10).

To curse someone is not only to declare a wish that the person suffer harm, but to revile or speak evil of that person.

"Honour thy father and thy mother: and, Thou shalt love thy neighbour as thyself" (Matthew 19:19).

"Honour thy father and mother; which is the first commandment with promise" (Ephesians 6:2).

To dishonor someone is to treat the person as common or menial or to shame or humiliate that person. Honor can be expressed in our thoughts, words, or deeds but always originates from the heart. If we honor others in words or deeds only and not from a pure heart, we are not in unity within ourselves and so are operating in sin. Honor must flow from a pure heart. We must forgive those who have hurt us, pray for them with passion, and want only the best for them.

Jesus set the ultimate example for us regarding obedience and honor. He said he did nothing on His own, but always did the will of His Father.

"Then said Jesus unto them, When ye have lifted up the Son of man, then shall ye know that I am he, and that I do nothing of myself; but as my Father hath taught me, I speak these things. And he that sent me is with me: the Father hath not left me alone; for I do always <u>those things that please Him</u>" (John 8:28–29 KJV). [Emphasis mine]

"I can of mine own self do nothing: as I hear, I judge: and my judgment is just; <u>because I seek not mine own will, but the will of the Father which hath sent me</u>" (John 5:30 KJV). [Emphasis mine]

If you are having consistent problems in any area of life, the difficulty may originate in your past relationship with your mother, your father, or other persons who raised you. In other words, you may have a heart problem.

Do you have recurrent problems with relationships, addictions, promiscuity, finances, anger issues, or health? If so, you are concealing unforgiveness, judgments, damaged emotions, inner vows, or unmet needs involving one or both of your parents. There may also be a generational curse operating in your lineage, but I will address that topic in another lesson.

It is not too late to make things right with God and to walk in obedience, processing and letting go of your past hurts,and wounds. You have already taken the first step by beginning this study.

God has been calling, wooing you ever so gently with His love. He has begun to open your eyes to your hidden pain. Now you are pursuing this study to learn how to process your painful past. Ask God to show you the hidden sins of your heart, those areas where you dishonored your parents. He has said that when we call upon Him with all our hearts He will answer.

"For I know the thoughts that I think toward you, saith the Lord, thoughts of peace, and not of evil, to give you an expected end. Then shall ye call upon me, and ye shall go and pray unto me, and I will hearken unto you. And ye shall seek me, and find me, when ye shall search for me with all your heart. And I will be found of you, saith the Lord: and I will turn away your captivity, and I will gather you from all the nations, and from all the places whither I have driven you, saith the Lord; and I will bring you again into the place whence I caused you to be carried away captive" (Jeremiah 29:11–14 KJV).

As God reveals your heart to you, ask Him to forgive you for judging those who have caused you pain. Then release forgiveness to your parents or authority figures for whatever you have against them in your heart. God will honor your desire to please Him. He will release you from your past by revealing your hidden sins and will take the journey with you through the healing process.

If you are consistently failing in some aspect of life, you can be sure that you dishonored an authority figure somewhere in your past. It may have been your mother, your father, a stepparent, a grandparent, or another person who raised you and had the most influence on your life in your formative years. A repetitive problem that you cannot seem to conquer may reflect dysfunction in your relationships. The problem may be the inability to hold a job for any length of time, chemical dependence, an eating disorder, trouble keeping your commitment to God, anger or rage, a shopping, relationship, or sexual addiction, or multiple divorces. The list is endless. The root of your problem may be hidden deep in your heart, and you may not be aware of its source.

If your problem is chemical abuse, one of your authority figures may have abused alcohol or drugs. This abuse and dysfunction created chaos in the home where you grew up, leaving you with unmet needs and damaged emotions. Because this hidden pain simmered deep within your soul, unforgiveness festered against an authority figure. By holding this unprocessed pain and unforgiveness in your heart, you set yourself up as this person's judge. A generational curse may also be operating in your family, keeping you bound to the same patterns of dysfunction. But this is a subject for a later lesson.

Perhaps your father or another authority figure was physically, verbally, or mentally abusive. As a child, you did not know how to process this developing pain hidden deep within. Satan set you up to reap dysfunctional behavior patterns later in life, and the only way to tear down these strongholds is to apply the blood of Jesus to these hidden painful areas.

Be encouraged because God has provided a way out for you bought by Christ's blood!

How to Honor Authority

You may ask how could you honor your parents when they abused you physically, emotionally, or verbally. The answer is by forgiving them for the wrongs you received at their hands and asking God to forgive you for judging them. Forgiveness is not a feeling; it is a choice you make because of your obedience to God and your love for Him. By choosing to pray blessings upon those who have hurt you and to forgive them, you allow God to change your emotions and to transform these people.

You choose to honor them by forgiving them for the injustices they have done to you. By forgiving, you refuse to remain their judge or to hold them accountable for their abuse. Instead, you release them to God, who is the righteous judge. Things will not go well for you in any area where you dishonor them by disobedience, hatred, bitterness, rebellion, or resentment even if these sins are hidden in your heart and are not translated into action.

Our personal history helps determine our perception, and our perception translates into conception, those thoughts, words, and actions to which we give birth.

The way we perceive circumstances is a direct result of our attitude. We see everything in a certain way—either positively or negatively—because of a predetermined mind-set, and our perceptions may be incorrect.

Taking advantage of our Adamic nature, Satan will make sure we mistakenly perceive the actions of our parents or authority figures and fail to see how these actions were intended. Even if we had Christ Himself for a parent, our Adamic nature would still lead us to perceive His decisions as unfair. Our perception may cause us to feel the actions of others are unjust and to become angry with those we believe have wronged us.

Our perceptions are first formed by the homes in which we grow up. The way we see the world is based on a combination of all our experiences from conception to the present. Viewing the question from this perspective, we begin to realize that our reality may not be the truth, but merely life as we know it. Everyone has different experiences, creating different perspectives on life. However, although many of our experiences differ, many are parallel.

The Word of God is the only means of measuring truth. Our perception of reality may well be a deviation from God's truth. It is imperative that we learn what God says regarding wholeness so we will not deceived by Satan and his demonic forces.

Various factors set our version of reality apart from the truth. In attempting to determine the truth, we often fail to consider the feelings of others or how they see things. Having a carnal or sinful nature, we human beings have a strong tendency to selfishness. We want our way; we want others to make us feel good, to give us an emotional fix, and to keep us from hurting.

The middle shield in the "Shield of Faith" illustration represents the soul, and the honey comb represents all of our experiences, starting from conception. Each hexagon represents a positive or a negative experience. Each experience is placed in the subconscious as a memory and remains there; every emotion raised by an experience also resides there.

Our perceptions and the contents of our subconscious will determine our future. Our characters, personalities, and reactions to life's situations result from this history. Not only are we the sum total of all our experiences, but we are also a product of our genetics. Let us not forget that genetics plays an important role in who we are and what we become.

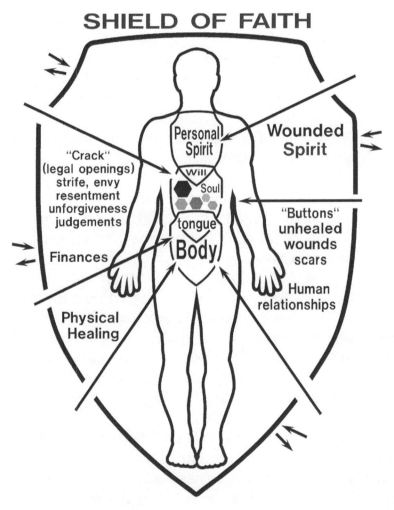

Illustration 3 – Shield of Faith

Who we become can be changed if we learn and apply the principles found in the Word of God that will set us free. That's what this study is all about—processing the past and exposing the hidden sins that cause cracks in the shield of faith, allowing Satan to "sift us as wheat" and keeping us from becoming all that we can be in Christ our Savior.

***All that you achieve and all that you fail to achieve
is the direct result of your own thoughts.
—James Allen***

Anger

> Be ye angry, and sin not: let not the sun go down upon
> your wrath: Neither give place to the devil.
> —Ephesians 4:26–27

In *Who Switched Off My Brain?*, Dr. Caroline Leaf writes, "Behavior starts with a thought. Thoughts stimulate emotions that then result in attitude and finally produce behavior. This symphony of electrochemical reactions in the body affects the way we think and feel physically. Therefore, toxic thoughts produce toxic emotions, which produce toxic attitudes, resulting in toxic behavior."

Anger encompasses annoyance, irritation, fury, rage, antagonism, and resentment. In and of itself, anger is not sinful, but involves our whole being—body (five senses) and soul (mind, will, and emotions). It can be our friend because it alerts us to wrong done to us. To ensure strong emotional, mental, and spiritual health, we must not only recognize anger when it occurs, but also know how to process this anger in a godly way. Anger becomes sin when we stew over an offense and repeat our displeasure to others.

Anger thrives and grows on unmet needs and damaged emotions. The basic psychological need to be loved, valued, and affirmed exists in all of us. If this need is not met, emotional distress and hidden anger issues result.

31

If we feel rejected, forgotten, ignored, mistreated, unaccepted, or unaffirmed by others, we may experience anger without realizing it. The longer we go without our emotional needs being met the angrier we become. This is especially true when someone significant in our lives ignores these needs.

If anger remains hidden and unprocessed, it will turn into resentment, bitterness, and unforgiveness and develop roots. If the cycle continues, it will produce dysfunctional character or personality traits. Left unchecked this will result in a hard heart, a wounded spirit, a perfectionist personality, rage, addictions, or promiscuity. Those who have denied and suppressed their feelings for too long may not be aware of who they are much less how they feel.

Toxic thoughts and emotions disturb the body's delicate chemical and electrical balance, damaging basic cell structure. These changes upset the body's function, doing mental and spiritual as well as physical harm. The person's immune system is compromised.

The Word tells us that if we obey God's laws and seek Him for direction in everything we do, our obedience will bring us health and peace. "My son, forget not my law; but let thine heart keep my commandments: For length of days, and long life, and peace, shall they add to thee" (Proverbs 3:1–2).

Toxic thoughts that we cover up never go away, but lie buried deep in the subconscious mind, or the soul realm, producing automatic reactions when an outside stimulus activates these memories. This is what I call a "button pushing" response.

Your mind perceives suppressed emotion as fear. Remember that fear is of Satan.

If we do not immediately forgive a hurt inflicted on us, we will rehearse the wrong in our minds. The Bible calls this meditation on the event. This meditation gives Satan an opening that allows him to torment our souls. That is what Scripture means by "giving place to the devil." We step out from underneath the protection of the blood of Jesus Christ and into Satan's territory.

Each time we rehearse an event, we inflict on ourselves the same emotional pain that we originally experienced. Scientific evidence shows that the brain does not know the difference between the original event and the imagined one. We go through the same anger, rejection, or humiliation we first felt.

These negative emotions produce unhealthy biochemical changes in the blood that will affect every cell in the body as the blood delivers toxins to these cells. This will eventually weaken the immune system. Our autonomic nervous system, the heart, the lungs, and the digestive tract will also affected. It takes seventy-two hours to neutralize and wash toxins out of our bodies. Therefore, if we do not forgive quickly, but continue to stew over wrongs real or imagined and tell others about them, we are slowly poisoning ourselves. This process allows sickness to come upon us and opens the door for Satan to enter our lives.

"For where envying and strife is, there is confusion and every evil work" (James 3:16).

Strife is sin and left unchecked it takes up residence in the heart, creating an open door for demonic activity in our lives.

- **✗** If feelings have not been experienced, expressed, or released, they will lodge within your soul realm and remain there until they are called forth to serve in your present circumstances. (And they will surface with a vengeance! Remember that sin is progressive.)
- **✗** Your reactions to problems, circumstances, or relationships are based on experiences that have been programmed onto your subconscious.
- **✗** Rebellion can result from repressed anger over rejection.

✖ All addictive behavior is motivated by the desire to pursue, to relieve, or to avoid a feeling.

The Enemy is a sly one. He will project toxic thoughts into your mind to see if you will buy into his lies. If he can get you to dwell on these thoughts, he knows the next step will be destructive actions on your part. Remember that what you allow yourself to meditate upon sooner or later translates into action.

He will constantly try to persuade you that others have negative intentions when the truth may be exactly the opposite. He will tell you that your spouse doesn't love you, that your boss doesn't like you, that you are not as good as everyone else, that you're not worthy of God's love, or that God can't possibly use you due to your past sins.

Satan's intention is to destroy your unity not only with others, but with yourself. He knows well that failing to walk in love and harmony with yourself and others will eventually wreak havoc in every area of your life. Remember James 3:16:"For where envying and strife is, there is confusion and every evil work."

Do not let Satan deceive you. With the blood of Jesus applied to those areas that need healing, you can be whole. God can and will use you despite your past. He will take the very situations Satan intended for your destruction and turn them around for your good. That is why you must constantly spend time in the Word of God and in prayer, allowing Him to change you into a reflection of Himself.

"But even unto this day, when Moses is read, the veil is upon their heart. Nevertheless when it shall turn to the Lord, the veil shall be taken away. Now the Lord is that Spirit: and where the Spirit of the Lord is, there is liberty. But we all, with open face beholding as in a glass the glory of the Lord, are changed into the same image from glory to glory, even as by the Spirit of the Lord." (2 Corinthians 3:15–18 KJV).

"Therefore seeing we have this ministry, as we have received mercy, we faint not; But have renounced the hidden things of dishonesty, not walking in craftiness, nor handling the word of God deceitfully; but by manifestation of the truth commending ourselves to every man's conscience in the sight of God. But if our gospel be hid, it is hid to them that are lost: In whom the god of this world hath blinded the minds of them which believe not, lest the light of the glorious gospel of Christ, who is the image of God, should shine unto them." (2 Corinthians 4:1–4 KJV).

To break the cycle of anger, you must first recognize that you have been in denial and are harboring suppressed anger. The only way you can accomplish this is to ask God to show you the hidden anger in your life.

Remember that life is all about decisions and choices. You must decide to be honest about the circumstances that produced the anger. A trained Christian counselor can help guide you through this process. If one is not available, you can talk to your prayer partner, to a clergy member, or to someone who will keep your confidence as well as affirm you in this process.

After acknowledging the source of your anger and pain, you must make the decision to forgive. This does not validate the wrong done to you, but instead releases you from holding a grudge while allowing you to gain right standing with God your Father. Do not forget to ask Him to forgive you for harboring unforgiveness in your heart toward the person who hurt you.

The final step is to pray for the person or persons who harmed or hurt you. God said in His Word to forgive those who have hurt you, to bless and not to curse them. By being obedient to His Word in this final step, you will allow God to heal your anger and your pain.

"That, in reference to your former manner of life, you lay aside the old self, which is being corrupted in accordance with the lusts of deceit, and that you be renewed in the spirit of your mind, and put on the new self, which in the likeness of God has been created in righteousness and holiness of the truth. Therefore, laying aside falsehood, speak truth, each one of you, with his neighbor, for we are members of one another. Be angry, and yet do not sin; do not let the sun go down on your anger, and do not give the devil an opportunity" (Ephesians 4:22–27 NASB).

I highly recommend Gary Chapman's book *Anger: Handling a Powerful Emotion in a Healthy Way* for further study on the subject of anger.

Bitterness

Looking diligently lest any man fail of the grace of God; lest any root of bitterness springing up trouble you, and thereby many be defiled.

—Hebrews 12:15 KJV

Bitterness is produced by something "distasteful or distressing to the mind" and may be "accompanied by severe pain or suffering." This feeling may include "intense animosity" and be "marked by cynicism and rancor," according to *Merriam Webster's Collegiate Dictionary Tenth Edition.*

Bitterness is the result of anger that we have allowed to grow unabated in our soul realm. If this anger is not acknowledged, then processed in a godly manner, it will continue to grow as a seed planted in the soil. Every time we speak to another person about an injustice we have suffered or brood over pain inflicted upon us, we water this seed of bitterness. If left to grow, it will produce a harvest of dysfunction in every aspect of our lives.

This word for *bitterness* in Hebrew means a poison; the word *springing* in this Scripture verse denotes germination, growth, and a sprouting. Therefore the picture painted here is that bitterness plants a seed of unforgiveness deep with us that produces the fruit of dysfunctional behavioral patterns later in our lives and causes us to reap similar circumstances in our relationships.

Forgiveness/Unforgiveness

> He hath not dealt with us after our sins; nor rewarded
> us according to our iniquities. For as the heaven is high
> above the earth, so great is his mercy toward them that
> fear him. As far as the east is from the west, so far hath he
> removed our transgressions from us. Like as a father pitieth
> his children, so the Lord pitieth them that fear him.
>
> —Psalm 103:10–13 KJV

By choosing to forgive, we let go of an offense, do not hold it against another, and forgo vengeance against that person. We choose not to talk about the offense with anyone but God and perhaps a close friend or a counselor. By forgiving, we allow God to change our emotions so that we want the best for the person who has hurt us.

When God made Adam and Eve and placed them in the garden of Eden, they were perfect. Created in His image, they were without sin. Therefore God walked with them, and talked with them face to face in the cool of the evening.

"So God created man in his own image, in the image of God created he him; male and female created he them" (Genesis 1:27 KJV).

All men and women have needed their sins forgiven since the fall of Adam and Eve. God told Adam he could eat of every tree in the garden except the Tree of Knowledge of Good and Evil. God said that if he ate of this tree he would surely die. The second chapter of Genesis offers this account.

Adam and Eve's sin had to be covered. Therefore God for the first time slew an animal to provide them clothing to hide their nakedness. "Unto Adam also and to his wife did the Lord God make coats of skins, and clothed them" (Genesis 3:21).

"And Aaron shall lay both his hands upon the head of the live goat, and confess over him all the iniquities of the children of Israel, and all their transgressions in all their sins, putting them upon the head of the goat, and shall send him away by the hand of a fit man into the wilderness: And the goat shall bear upon him all their iniquities unto a land not inhabited: and he shall let go the goat in the wilderness" (Leviticus 16:21–22).

These two verses present the fundamental Old Testament idea that forgiveness is not the remission of a penalty, but the separation of the sinner from his sin. This atonement was good for only one year and then had to be repeated all over again. Aaron confessed Israel's sins over the goat, and the goat was led out into the wilderness to signify the separation of the people of Israel from their transgressions. In contrast, Christ took our sins upon His own body when He died on the cross of Calvary. This event will never occur again because He became the eternal scapegoat for us.

Jesus paid the price for us. The Word says, "According as His divine power hath given unto us all things that pertain unto life and godliness, through the knowledge of him that hath called us to glory and virtue" (2 Peter 1:3).

"He who did not withhold his own Son, but gave him up for all of us, will he not with him also give us everything else?" (Romans 8:32).

"Who forgiveth all thine iniquities; who healeth all thy diseases; who redeemeth thy life from destruction; who crowneth thee with lovingkindness and tender mercies; who satisfieth thy mouth with good things; so that thy youth is renewed like the eagle's" (Psalm 103:3– 5).

"Surely he hath borne our griefs, and carried our sorrows: yet we did esteem him stricken, smitten of God, and afflicted. But he was wounded for our transgressions, he was bruised for our iniquities: the chastisement of our peace was upon him; and with his stripes we are healed. All we like sheep have gone astray; we have turned everyone to his own way; and the Lord hath laid on him the iniquity of us all. He was oppressed, and he was afflicted, yet he opened not his mouth: he is brought as a lamb to the slaughter, and as a sheep before her shearers is dumb, so he openeth not his mouth. He was taken from prison and from judgment: and who shall declare his generation? for he was cut off out of the land of the living: for the transgression of my people was he stricken" (Isaiah 53:4–8).

God made a new covenant with humanity after the death and resurrection of Jesus, His Son.

"For this is the covenant that I will make with the house of Israel after those days, saith the Lord; I will put my laws into their mind, and write them in their hearts: and I will be to them a God, and they shall be to me a people: And they shall not teach every man his neighbour, and every man his brother, saying, Know the Lord: for all shall know me, from the least to the greatest. For I will be merciful to their unrighteousness, and their sins and their iniquities will I remember no more" (Hebrews 8:10–12).

In Isaiah 43:25, again God said, "I, even I, am he that blotteth out thy transgressions for mine own sake, and will not remember thy sins." (Emphasis mine)

God said He would cast our sins into the sea to remember them no more. Isn't that just like our loving, patient heavenly Father? "He will turn again, he will have compassion upon us; he will subdue our iniquities; and thou wilt cast all their sins into the depths of the sea" (Micah 7:19).

Even after we get saved, we are still not perfect, just forgiven. "But if we walk in the light, as he is in the light, we have fellowship one with another, and the blood of Jesus Christ his Son cleanseth us from all sin. If we say that we have no sin, we deceive ourselves, and the truth is not in us. If we confess our sins, he is faithful and just to forgive us our sins, and to cleanse us from all unrighteousness" (1 John 1:7– 9).

If we sin, God has made provision for us to receive forgiveness and continue to serve Him, as this verse shows. "My little children, these things write I unto you, that ye sin not. And if any man sin, we have an advocate with the Father, Jesus Christ the righteous" (1 John 2:1).

"There is therefore now no condemnation to them which are in Christ Jesus, who walk not after the flesh, but after the Spirit" (Romans 8:1).

If your mind still brings up past sins, you can see now where these thoughts come from. They don't come from God, but from Satan or perhaps from your own troubled soul because you have not forgiven others or yourself even though God has forgiven you.

According to Philippians 4:8, we can control our thought life: "Finally, brethren, whatsoever things are true, whatsoever things are honest, whatsoever things are just, whatsoever things are pure, whatsoever things are lovely, whatsoever things are of good report: if there be any virtue, and if there be any praise, think on these things."

Our hidden or unrealized unforgiveness of others is a door that Satan uses to enter our minds and cause discord in our relationships. God has no choice but to let Satan disrupt and demean our lives and cause us despair, because God will not violate His own Word.

Unforgiveness is sin! Sin always brings forth death in one form or another. Whether it is in the dying relationship of a husband and a wife, a broken friendship, a business or financial failure, or a church split, the result is still the same: the loss of a blessing that God has tried to establish in our lives. Sin is always the open door for Satan to kill, steal, and destroy.

> Therefore is the kingdom of heaven likened unto a certain king, which would take account of his servants. And when he had begun to reckon, one was brought unto him, which owed him ten thousand talents. But

40

forasmuch as he had not to pay, his lord commanded him to be sold, and his wife, and children, and all that he had, and payment to be made. The servant therefore fell down, and worshipped him, saying, Lord, have patience with me, and I will pay thee all.

Then the lord of that servant was moved with compassion, and loosed him, and forgave him the debt.

But the same servant went out, and found one of his fellow servants, which owed him an hundred pence: and he laid hands on him, and took him by the throat, saying, Pay me that thou owest. And his fellow servant fell down at his feet, and besought him, saying, Have patience with me, and I will pay thee all. And he would not: but went and cast him into prison, till he should pay the debt.

So when his fellow servants saw what was done, they were very sorry and came and told unto their lord all that was done.

Then his lord, after that he had called him, said unto him, O thou wicked servant, I forgave thee all that debt, because thou desiredst me: Shouldest not thou also have had compassion on thy fellow servant, even as I had pity on thee? And his lord was wroth, and delivered him to the tormentors, till he should pay all that was due unto him.

So likewise shall my heavenly Father do also unto you, if ye from your hearts forgive not everyone his brother their trespasses. (Matthew 18:23–35)

"For if ye forgive men their trespasses, your heavenly Father will also forgive you: But if ye forgive not men their trespasses, neither will your Father forgive your trespasses" (Matthew 6:14–15).

Unforgiveness binds our sins to us as well as to others.

"Verily I say unto you, Whatsoever ye shall bind on earth shall be bound in heaven; and whatsoever ye shall loose on earth shall be loosed in heaven" (Matthew 18:18).

"Be not deceived for God is not mocked, Whatsoever a man soweth that shall he also reap" (Galatians 6:7).

When we hold unforgiveness in our hearts toward someone, we are destined to reap the same situation again through those we love, whether it is a spouse, a friend, or an employer.

"Therefore thou art inexcusable, O man, whosoever thou art that judgest: for wherein thou judgest another, thou condemnest thyself; for thou that judgest doest the same things" (Romans 2:1).

The very thing we have judged someone else for having done we ourselves will do or will reap from others. There is no way around this. The Word never lies but always comes to pass.

It is easy to blame others for our recurring problems. That way we pass the responsibility for change on to someone else. As long as another person is to blame, we do not have to change or assume the responsibility for doing so. But the Word says it is we, not our brother, who must change.

"Why do you see the speck in your neighbor's eye, but do not notice the log in your own eye? Or how can you say to your neighbor, 'Let me take the speck out of your eye,' while the log is in your own eye? You hypocrite, first take the log out of your own eye, and then you will see clearly to take the speck out of your neighbor's eye" (Matthew 7:3–5).

The blame game began in the garden. Adam and Eve also had a knack for blaming someone else and denying responsibility for their own actions. When God asked Adam what he had done, he said it was "that woman you gave me" who made him partake of the apple. Eve told God "it was the serpent" who tempted her to eat.

Adam and Eve had free will and could choose obedience to God just as we can today. They chose instead to listen to the serpent and do the very thing their Father had commanded them not to do, suffering the consequences as a result. We also have a choice about whether we will forgive others when they hurt our feelings or offend us.

Sometimes we do not even perceive that we harbor unforgiveness against those who hurt or offend us. We are so accustomed to denying our anger, frustration, or other feelings that even as adults we remain in denial. This denial became a way of survival learned early in childhood. The Holy Spirit brings the sins concealed in our hearts to light only when we cry out to Him to do this.

"The heart is deceitful above all things, and desperately wicked: who can know it?

I the Lord search the heart, I try the reins, even to give every man according to his ways, and according to the fruit of his doings." (Jeremiah 17:9–10 KJV).

The Holy Spirit is so gentle that He will not violate our will in any way. We must invite Him into our hearts daily to remove all the hidden sins of unforgiveness. He will not bully us into examining these veiled places in our hearts. Satan works by trying to get us to do things against our wills, but our loving Father would never do this.

We must daily ask God to reveal to us the hidden sins of unforgiveness in our hearts. This is not the same as asking God to forgive us our sins the way we did when we were born again. Rather, we should ask God to search the recesses of our souls and reveal all those hidden things that keep us from becoming all He has called us to be.

In Psalm 139:23-24, King David pleaded, "Search me, O God, and know my heart: try me, and know my thoughts: And see if there be any wicked way in me, and lead me in the way everlasting."

Alone with his sheep in the fields, David prayed to become all that God had called him to be. The only way we can become all that God has called us to be is by taking responsibility for our situations, by asking God to show us our hearts, and by resisting the temptation to blame others for our circumstances.

Think back to situations in your past. Can you see any patterns that keep repeating themselves? If so, you can be sure there is unforgiveness somewhere deep in your heart that has its roots in your childhood. The only way to stop the cycle of hurt is to ask God to reveal to you your heart and the pains that caused the unforgiveness. Only then can you release the person or persons whom you feel harmed you and did you wrong. Ask God to forgive you for judging them and for holding unforgiveness in your heart toward them; release forgiveness to them for the wrongs they did to you.

Forgiveness is a choice, not a feeling. It is a decision you make to please God because you love Him and because His Word says to forgive. If you will be obedient to God's Word by releasing forgiveness to those who have offended you, God will do the rest by aligning your feelings with your forgiveness.

The feeling of forgiveness may not come overnight. It may take months or even years to accomplish in the fullness or it may be instantaneous. Do not despair. God will decide when to bring this feeling to pass in your life. Your obligation is to be obedient to His commands and to release forgiveness to those who have hurt you in any way.

To release forgiveness, you may have to repeat, perhaps many times, "Father, I forgive ___ for what he did to me." If the hurt has been festering for a long time, it may take quite a while for your feelings to follow suit. God has a lot of bitterness, anger, resentment, and possibly hate to work out of you. Do not give up, because God never gives up on us. His patience is never- ending. He will accomplish the work He has started in His own time.

"Take heed to yourselves: If thy brother trespass against thee, rebuke him; and if he repent, forgive him. And if he trespass against thee seven times in a day, and seven times in a day turn again to thee, saying, I repent; thou shalt forgive him" (Luke 17:3–4).

"Then said Jesus, Father, forgive them; for they know not what they do. And they parted his raiment, and cast lots" (Luke 23:34).

"Anyone whom you forgive, I also forgive. What I have forgiven, if I have forgiven anything, has been for your sake in the presence of Christ. And we do this so that we may not be outwitted by Satan; for we are not ignorant of his design" (2 Corinthians 2:10–11 NRSV).

"To whom ye forgive any thing, I forgive also: for if I forgave anything, to whom I forgave it, for your sakes forgave I it in the person of Christ; Lest Satan should get an advantage of us: for we are not ignorant of his devices." (Matthew 6:14–15 KJV).

"Have faith in God. For assuredly, I say to you, whoever says to this mountain, 'Be removed and cast into the sea,' and does not doubt in his heart, but believes that those things he says will come to pass, he will have whatever he says. Therefore I say to you, whatever things you ask when you pray, believe that you receive them, and you will have them. And whenever you stand praying, if you have anything against anyone, forgive him, that your Father in heaven may also forgive you your trespasses. But if you do not forgive, neither will your Father in heaven forgive your trespasses" (Mark 11:22–26 NKJV).

Reading this passage, we want to concentrate only on the first part and forget about the second. We want to believe the part that says God will remove mountains if only we believe. We prefer to ignore the last two verses, which declare that for this to happen we must walk in forgiveness and love; the power of faith depends upon our ability to forgive others just as Jesus took our sins upon His own person, died for us, and rose again.

"For we through the Spirit wait for the hope of righteousness by faith.

For in Jesus Christ neither circumcision availeth any thing, nor uncircumcision; but faith which worketh by love." (Galatians 5:5–6 KJV).

> *Forgiveness is a decision and has nothing to do*
> *with feelings. It is a choice, an act of your will.*

"Recompense to no man evil for evil. Provide things honest in the sight of all men.
If it be possible, as much as lieth in you, live peaceably with all men.
Dearly beloved, avenge not yourselves, but rather give place unto wrath: for it is written, Vengeance is mine; I will repay, saith the Lord. Therefore if thine enemy hunger, feed him; if he thirst, give him drink: for in so doing thou shalt heap coals of fire on his head.
Be not overcome of evil, but overcome evil with good." (Romans 12:17–21 KJV).

When we feel that someone has done us wrong, our first inclination is to exact revenge any way we can; to pay this person back for the injustice inflicted upon us; to tell everyone of this injustice; to punish the person for hurting us. As we can see, not only in the above verses, but throughout the Bible, God demands that we walk in forgiveness daily. He does not want us to get back at others for the wrongs they have inflicted upon us.

"Likewise, ye husbands, dwell with them according to knowledge, giving honour unto the wife, as unto the weaker vessel, and as being heirs together of the grace of life; that your prayers be not hindered" (1 Peter 3:7 KJV).

We sometimes wonder why our prayers are not answered. Could the reason be that we have hidden unforgiveness somewhere deep in our hearts? Strife, discord, or disunity between ourselves and others could be the cause of unanswered prayers. These manifestations of the flesh are sins and an instant doorway for Satan and his demonic forces to gain access to our lives.

"That he would grant you, according to the riches of his glory, to be strengthened with might by his Spirit in the inner man;
That Christ may dwell in your hearts by faith; that ye, being rooted and grounded in love,
May be able to comprehend with all saints what is the breadth, and length, and depth, and height;
And to know the love of Christ, which passeth knowledge, that ye might be filled with all the fulness of God." (Ephesians 3:16–19 KJV).

To be rooted in the love of Christ, we must walk daily in forgiveness of those who have offended or harmed us in any way. Otherwise, we have opened the doors of our hearts to Satan to wreak havoc in our lives.

Forgiveness does not negate our God-given right to set appropriate boundaries. We must exercise this right so that others cannot abuse us. God does not want us abused! In Matthew 22, Jesus says we are not only to love God, but to love our neighbors as ourselves. How can we love ourselves and let others abuse us in any way?

"Jesus said unto him, Thou shalt love the Lord thy God with all thy heart, and with all thy soul, and with all thy mind. This is the first and great commandment. And the second is like unto it, Thou shalt love thy neighbour as thyself" (Matthew 22:37–39 KJV).

Judgment

Therefore thou art inexcusable, O man, whosoever
thou art that judgest: for wherein thou judgest another,

> thou condemnest thyself; for thou that judgest doest the
> same thing.
>
> —Romans 2:1 KJV

> Judge not, that ye be not judged. For with what judgment
> ye judge, ye shall be judged: and with what measure ye
> mete, it shall be measured to you again. And why beholdest
> thou the mote that is in thy brother's eye, but considerest
> not the beam that is in thine own eye? Or how wilt thou say
> to thy brother, Let me pull out the mote out of thine eye;
> and, behold, a beam is in thine own eye? Thou hypocrite,
> first cast out the beam out of thine own eye; and then shalt
> thou see clearly to cast out the mote out of thy brother's eye.
>
> —Matthew 7:1–5 KJV

It is easy to point out someone else's faults and to ignore our own. By focusing on others, we ignore accountability for our own actions. When we judge others, we validate ourselves in our own eyes. By putting others down, we lift ourselves to a higher plane, not only in own minds but in the minds of others, or so we think.

If we focus on the faults of others, we do not have to admit our own shortcomings or change anything about ourselves. After all, look how good we are and how bad the other person is. Talk about self-validation and pride!

"You just don't know what happened to me as a child," you may be saying. "You don't know the abuse I suffered at the hands of others who were supposed to love and protect me; you don't know the broken relationships and rejection I've endured; you don't know the mental, verbal, or physical pain I've had to suffer through." You are right. But I do know through my own experiences that Jesus indeed came to set captives free, to liberate them from broken hearts and relationships, from suppressed pain and sorrows, and from bondages developed in childhood so that can experience the joy and the peace that only God can give.

When Jesus was in the temple, He opened the scroll and declared, "The Spirit of the Lord is upon me, because he hath anointed me to preach the gospel to the poor; he hath sent me to heal the brokenhearted, to preach deliverance to the captives, and recovering of sight to the blind, to set at liberty them that are bruised, to preach the acceptable year of the Lord" (Luke 4:18–19 KJV).

There is hope for the hurting! That hope lies in the cross of Jesus. Healing lies in the blood and in the name of Christ. While salvation is free, wholeness takes determination, perseverance, self-denial, study, and a willingness to let go of the past and our self-will.

The decision is all ours. With His death and resurrection, Jesus paid the price for all of humanity's sins, whether they be emotional, physical, spiritual, or financial. God told Moses to tell the children of Israel "I am that I am" had sent him (Exodus 3:14 KJV). That says it all. The rest is up to us.

> Beware of false prophets, which come to you in sheep's clothing, but inwardly they are ravening wolves. Ye shall know them by their fruits. Do men gather grapes of thorns, or figs of thistles? Even so every good tree bringeth forth good fruit; but a corrupt tree bringeth forth evil fruit. A good tree cannot bring forth evil fruit, neither can a corrupt tree bring forth good fruit.
>
> Every tree that bringeth not forth good fruit is hewn down, and cast into the fire. Wherefore by their fruits ye shall know them.
>
> Not every one that saith unto me, Lord, Lord, shall enter into the kingdom of heaven; but he that doeth the will of my Father which is in heaven.
>
> Many will say to me in that day, Lord, Lord, have we not prophesied in thy name? and in thy name have cast out devils? and in thy name done many wonderful works?

And then will I profess unto them, I never knew you: depart from me, ye that work iniquity.

Therefore whosoever heareth these sayings of mine, and doeth them, I will liken him unto a wise man, which built his house upon a rock: And the rain descended, and the floods came, and the winds blew, and beat upon that house; and it fell not: for it was founded upon a rock.

And every one that heareth these sayings of mine, and doeth them not, shall be likened unto a foolish man, which built his house upon the sand: And the rain descended, and the floods came, and the winds blew, and beat upon that house; and it fell: and great was the fall of it. (Matthew 7:15-27 KJV)

In this same chapter of Matthew, where Jesus told the multitudes to "judge not that they be not judged," He also told them to beware of false prophets. (In Hebrew, the term means a pretended foreteller or a religious impostor.) He warned them not to be deceived by Satan operating in others, but to be discerning of the evil spirits doing this. The Word of God requires us to judge sin and to call it what it is: sin.

We are to be diligent in our walk with the Creator, ever attentive to the wiles of the Enemy, because the Word of God states unequivocally that not all who say "Lord Lord" will enter the kingdom of God. From the beginning of time to our own day, false teachers have abounded, saying one thing in public and doing another behind closed doors.

God warns us, "And we beseech you, brethren, to know them which labor among you, and are over you in the Lord, and admonish you" (1 Thessalonians 5:12).

In Hebrew, the word *know* is sometimes used to imply our knowledge beforehand of those who speak into our lives. We are not to allow just anyone to lay hands praying or prophesying over us. We are to be aware, consider, be sure, and know their walk with God. When we ask for prayer, our spirit is open to receiving from the person ministering to us. Whatever spirit the person ministering contains,good or bad, will ultimately transfer into us.

The Word tells us that wolves in sheep's clothing will appear. Clean on the outside, they are full of uncleanness, hypocrisy, and iniquity on the inside.

"Woe unto you, scribes and Pharisees, hypocrites! for ye are like unto whited sepulchres, which indeed appear beautiful outward, but are within full of dead men's bones, and of all uncleanness. Even so ye also outwardly appear righteous unto men, but within ye are full of hypocrisy and iniquity" (Matthew 23:27–28 KJV).

We must be aware of these deceiving and self-centered persons. These people have only one goal in life: to draw attention to how great and wonderful they are. This is the sin that caused Lucifer to fall from his place in heaven before God created Adam and Eve. This is the sin of pride.

We are to be diligent, watchful, and aware and prayerfully consider those we allow to influence our lives.

Inner Vow

An inner vow is an unyielding facet of our habitual ways of the flesh. This directive sent to our inner being thereafter controls and blocks its energies and actions.

"Come now, you who say, 'Today or tomorrow, we shall go to such and such a city, and spend a year there and engage in business and make a profit.' Yet you do not know what your life will be like tomorrow. You are just a vapor that appears for a little while and then vanishes away.

Instead, you ought to say, 'If the Lord wills, we shall live and also do this or that'" (James 4:13–15 NASB).

"But I say unto you, Swear not at all; neither by heaven; for it is God's throne: Nor by the earth; for it is his footstool: neither by Jerusalem; for it is the city of the great King. Neither shalt thou swear by thy head, because thou canst not make one hair white or black. But let your communication be, Yea, yea; Nay, nay: for whatsoever is more than these cometh of evil" (Matthew 5:34–37 KJV). The word *swear* in Hebrew is *omnuo*, meaning to take or to declare an oath.

A heart of stone includes inner vows. The Bible does not specially mention them, but speaks of stubbornness, stony hearts, and rebelliousness.

"Harden not your heart, as in the provocation, and as in the day of temptation in the wilderness: When your fathers tempted me, proved me, and saw my work. Forty years long was I grieved with this generation, and said, It is a people that do err in their heart, and they have not known my ways: Unto whom I sware in my wrath that they should not enter into my rest" (Psalm 95:8–11 KJV).

By the time they are six years old, people have usually made inner vows. They can also make them later in life without knowing it. This can happen when something or someone causes pain and a person makes an inner vow never to let the situation occur again.

The mind blocks out those things that contradict the inner vows we have made. Inner vows become obstructions in our nature that force us to feel, think, and act according to the mold these vows have set. They block out the Holy Spirit in the particular area of a vow.

Inner vows refuse to be changed. We may naturally mature out of childish ways and find ourselves free of many things through conversion or counsel. However, inner vows do not so easily surrender their hold upon us.

In their book *Prenatal Wounds and Sins*, the Reverends John and Paula Sandford of Elijah House Ministries offer the example of a woman who continuously miscarried boy babies. After much counseling with the Sandfords, she remembered growing up with vicious brothers who had cruelly mistreated her. Therefore, when she was about ten or twelve, she had made an inner vow that she would never have a boy child. The Sandfords told her the only way to be released from her vow was to forgive her brothers for inflicting pain and humiliation upon her.

You must remove the root of sin. You must ask forgiveness for making the vow, cover it with the blood of Jesus and bring it to the cross of Christ, then release yourself to be all God has called you to be in the area of the vow. This is important.

You can attend counseling to help deal with a problem. There you will learn expected behavior patterns in given situations. You may be much better for a few weeks and be capable of changing your ways. Then you may begin to slide right back into your old behavior patterns as an inner vow exerts its power.

Inner vows require recognition. The only way to break them is through the name and the blood of Jesus. You must see them by faith. You must persevere.

Not all inner vows are negative. But these vows only coerce you into good habits and fleshly righteousness. These vows too must be broken. When you make vows, however well intended, you set yourself up to operate in the flesh when you should rely on God for the strength to do better.

For example, young boys in certain homes learn early in life never to hit a girl or to use foul language in front of one. The boy may make a vow to be just like Daddy, who has never done these things with Mommy. Such a vow often coerces the male into fleshly righteousness, preventing him from having a productive emotional fight with his wife later in life. People need to have healthy discussions and talk things over.

Do you recognize yourself in any of these illustrations? If so, there is help and hope for you. Ask God to forgive you for the sin of having a hard heart or of making an inner vow. Ask Him to create a heart that is pure and that seeks God's will and the truth of His Word.

"Create in me a clean heart, O God; and renew a right spirit within me" (Psalm 51:10 KJV).

God is ever-present and ready to forgive you and to restore all the things missing in your life.

The decision to make an inner vow is usually the result of someone or something that has caused you pain. Because of the tremendous emotional or physical suffering you endured, you want at all costs to keep this from happening again.

When you make an inner vow, whether you remember it or not, you have set yourself up as a mini god in the area of the vow. You declare that you will control this area of your life. This is sin. You have become your own idol. This inner vow will open the door of your heart and allow Satan to bring destruction to your life in the area where the oath originated.

The inner vow can go one of two ways. It can bind you to repeat the very thing you hate or it can cause you to go to the extreme in the opposite direction. Either way you become powerless over your reactions in similar circumstances.

A mother had several children and was very sickly, leaving most of the responsibility for the household and for the younger children to her eldest daughter. This situation created a void in the girl's life since she could no longer simply be a child.

As she grew up bearing a tremendous responsibility for a girl her age, she made an inner vow that she would never have children. When she got married her life was good except in one area. She and her husband wanted children, but for some unknown reason she was unable to conceive. They saw every doctor they could find, but to no avail. None could find any biological reason either of them could not conceive.

As a result, the lady went to Reverend Sanford for counseling where God revealed to John the reason for her barrenness.

The Holy Spirit told John her problem resulted from the inner vow she had made as a young girl. This vow was so strong that it controlled her reproductive organs and kept her from conceiving. So John led her in a prayer, asking God to forgive her for the inner vow, bringing the sin under the blood of the cross of Calvary and rendering it null and void. The woman was set free. She then confessed the Word of God over herself, speaking wholeness to her body as God had created it.

Not long after this session, she was able to conceive. She and her husband had several more children.

Heart of Stone

> Then will I sprinkle clean water upon you, and ye shall be clean: from all your filthiness, and from all your idols, will I cleanse you. A new heart also will I give you, and a new spirit will I put within you: and I will take away the stony heart out of your flesh, and I will give you a heart of flesh. And I will put my spirit within you, and cause you to walk in my statutes, and ye shall keep my judgments, and do them.
>
> —Ezekiel 36:25–27 KJV

To keep from experiencing pain, we build defensive walls, hardening our hearts to protect ourselves. Once these walls are established, our reactions become automatic. We do not have to think about a response or make a conscience decision to protect ourselves in any situation threatening pain. Our perception and therefore our reactions are controlled by our painful past.

When we learned to walk and to talk as children, we had to think and to concentrate on what we were doing and how we would do it. Once we learned to walk, it became automatic.

In the same way, when we are hurt we put up walls around our hearts, encouraging protective reactions that are automatic in similar circumstances. Our original motive was to protect ourselves from being hurt in the same way again. But as a result, we have developed hard hearts and are no longer conscious of our dysfunctional reactions to others.

Our brains became hard-wired to react in certain ways in particular situations. The pathways we have fashioned in the thinking process have become involuntary reflexes.

A hard heart is the manifestation of hurt that has been hidden rather than acknowledged and processed in a godly manner. In failing to quickly release forgiveness to the person who hurt us, we have allowed the seed of unforgiveness to grow, creating a heart of stone deep within our soul realm.

This hard heart is the result of anger, resentment, bitterness, and full-blown unforgiveness that we have not dealt with in a Christ-like manner. The hard heart can also be a result of damaged emotions and of unmet needs for love, attention, and validation during our formative first six years of life. Because of these conditions, our spirit continues to grow more wounded.

Those of us who are new Christians must ask God to show us the areas of our hearts that have become hardened because of past pains. We must dig deep to the foundations of our defensive walls. After acknowledging that we have these walls, we must ask the Holy Spirit to reveal their exact nature. We must then bring that defensive wall, that automatic practice of the old nature, to the cross, get healed, and be freed of it.

Even in the best families, people have hearts of stone to some degree. Even those born into Christian homes have them. Their parents were human and carried pains from the past into their relationship unless they dealt with them before getting married and having children. Still, they are not perfect and will not have conquered all the hidden sins of the heart while in the flesh.

Another point to consider is that we are all born with a sinful nature and are capable of perceiving situations in error rather than as our parents intended. Our parents may have had our best interest at heart in any given situation, yet because of our sinful nature and our limited perspective, Satan made sure we saw everything in the worst light.

There are two principles to remember. First, hearts have more flexibility in families that show love, kindness, and respect and live with simplicity. Second, hearts are less flexible and more severe in families that do not show love, kindness, and respect, do not live with simplicity, and demand perfect behavior.

As a person grows up, a heart of stone will become obvious. People will say, "That guy is so hard- hearted he wouldn't do anything for anyone." It is important that we become aware of the possibility of a hidden heart of stone. A heart of stone is formed in childhood, and when we grow up, we not be aware that it exists.

When we allow a hard heart to grow deep within us as a result of unprocessed anger and pain, we put on counterfeit armor in an effort to protect ourselves from being hurt again. By failing to release forgiveness to those who have harmed us, we prevent others from getting past this armor to love us and can't escape our self-made prison to give others the love God intended us to offer them. We are bound in emotional chains by our sins and are not even aware of our condition.

No matter how good a spouse we have, this person can never do enough to make us feel loved as long as we maintain the wall we have constructed to protect ourselves from pain. The problem lies deep within each one of us, and only Christ can fill the void. Try as we might to fill it with alcohol, drugs, sex, relationships, or shopping, only Jesus can accomplish this tremendous task.

This wall also becomes a barrier between us and God. Our initial intent was to keep others from hurting us; we had no idea that we were also keeping God out of certain areas of our lives.

The way we saw male authority figures in our childhood is the same way we perceive God! Only by processing our emotional pains, releasing forgiveness, and asking God to forgive us for judging others can we begin to trust God and to see Him as the loving Father He is.

> Hear then the parable of the sower. When anyone hears the word of the kingdom, and does not understand it, the evil one comes and snatches away what has been sown in his heart. This is the one on whom seed was sown beside the road.
>
> And the one on whom seed was sown on the rocky places, this is the man who hears the word, and immediately receives it with joy; yet he has no firm root in himself, but is only temporary, and when affliction or persecution arises because of the word, immediately he falls away. And the one on whom seed was sown among the thorns, this is the man who hears the word, and the worry of the world, and the deceitfulness of riches choke the word, and it becomes unfruitful.
>
> And the one on whom seed was sown on the good soil, this is the man who hears the word and understands it; who indeed bears fruit, and brings forth, some a hundredfold, some sixty, and some thirty. (Matthew 13:18–23 NASB)

The sower is someone who teaches, preaches, or expounds upon the Word of God. As the Word is sowed, Christian hearts receive it; sometimes it falls by the wayside, sometimes on stony hearts, sometimes among thorns, and sometimes on good soil.

The phrase *beside the road* indicates the heart of the person was not prepared to receive the Word of God, since a roadside is usually hard, uncultivated, and incapable of producing crops or anything good. A roadside often consists of rocks. In other words, the person has not prepared his heart to receive the Word and so has not allowed it to grow and to nurture his soul and his spirit.

The rocky places point to a person who has not studied the Word of God and allowed it to show him his hidden sins and faults. This person may also be one who has sat under the Word of God all his life yet not allowed the light of the Holy Spirit to shine upon his pains, unforgiveness, and judgments. When troubles come, and they surely will, he is easily offended and leaves the church or even turns away from God. This person cannot seem to stay planted in one church for any length of time. He has never asked the Holy Spirit to show him his hidden sins and to cleanse him from all filthiness of the flesh. He has a hard heart yet blames everyone else for his misfortunes.

"Search me, O God, and know my heart; try me and know my anxious thoughts; and see if there be any hurtful way in me, and lead me in the everlasting way" (Psalm 139:23–24).

"Among the thorns" in Matthew 13:22 portrays a person who is self-indulgent, vain egotistical, selfish, conceited, extravagant in the pursuit of personal pleasure and unconcerned with anything but himself. This type of person is narcissistic.

"And take heed to yourselves, lest at any time your hearts be overcharged with surfeiting, and drunkenness, and cares of this life, and so that day come upon you unawares.

For as a snare shall it come on all them that dwell on the face of the whole earth." (Luke 21:34–35 KJV).

When the seed falls on good ground, a person has allowed the Holy Spirit to search every area of his being, helping him recognize and remove anything not pleasing to God. He is an ardent student of the Word of God and is dedicated, prayerful, unselfish, and humble. He repents easily, and his first love is Jesus.

He will quickly ask God to show him the hidden sins in his heart before he blames others for his circumstances. He takes responsibility for his actions, then pursues God relentlessly for the answers to his issues.

He is quick to forgive others for their transgressions and at the same time quiet capable of setting appropriate boundaries that others may not cross. He has a godly self-love that is healthy in every respect.

> *Unconditional love is a fire that will melt*
> *whatever remains of the heart of stone.*

Wounded/Slumbering Spirit

> The spirit of a man will sustain his infirmity; but a wounded spirit who can bear?
> —Proverbs 18:14 KJV

A wounded spirit results from a hurt or a wrong placed in the subconscious and allowed to remain. This hurt or wrong will grow, opening the person to reap in kind.

The subconscious is the mind of the spirit and retains all the memories and the emotions related to every wounding event, resulting in dysfunction in this area in all future relationships.

Each unprocessed wound in the spirit represents a hurting little girl or boy who has not matured in this area. When similar situations occur, we react based on the emotions of this hurting little girl or boy instead of responding in a mature Christian way. We respond not only to the present circumstance but to all past wounded feelings. Memories emerge with a vengeance, flooding us with pain and despair.

This overreaction to stimuli has pushed a button from our past. The brain does not differentiate between past and present events when painful emotions are produced not only by current circumstances but by earlier events.

In the midst of these overwhelming emotions, we can only see what another person has done to us, not realizing these feelings are a result of unfinished business deep within us. Our only hope is to ask God to show us our part in the situation—what lies hidden in our past that continues to yield the same scenario in our present relationships.

"A merry heart doeth good like a medicine: but a broken spirit drieth the bones" (Proverbs 17:22 KJV).

The bones contain bone marrow, which produces blood for the human body. The life of the body is in the blood. If the bones dried up, there would be no more life in the body. A wounded spirit can cause sickness that will eventually kill a person is left unchecked.

"Love does no wrong to a neighbor; love therefore is the fulfillment of the law. And this do, knowing the time, that it is already the hour for you to <u>awaken from sleep</u>; for now salvation is nearer to us than when we believed. The night is almost gone, and the day is at hand. Let us therefore lay aside the deeds of darkness and put on the armor of light" (Romans 13:10–12 NASB). [Emphasis mine]

The word for *sleep* in Hebrew relates to spiritual sleep, a dormant or inactive state. When our spirit becomes wounded and remains in this state, whether we are aware of this condition or not, the area of the wounding cannot reach godly maturity. The wounded spirit is sluggish, dull, and apathetic. It is only by approaching others in love, forgiving, and releasing blessings that we reach wholeness and maturity in our spirits.

God calls us to awake, to put off the manifestations of our flesh, and to stop reacting to people and circumstances out of our emotions. Instead He wants us to submit the hidden sinful areas of our soul realm to the illumination of the Holy Spirit and experience healing so we can respond in a Christ-like manner. The Holy Spirit wants to show us the hidden iniquities of our hearts that keep us from becoming all God has called us to be; He wants to walk with us through the journey to wholeness; He wants to encourage us to "hold fast our confession of faith and lay hold on eternal life."

Expectations

Based on our experiences, our hearts develop an expectation that life will go a certain way for us. This expectatation, created in the home where we grew up, continues into our adult years, affecting all of our present experiences and perceptions.

If we experienced abuse in any way, even if it was emotional neglect, we tend to believe that all fathers, mothers, or other authority figures are the same. Because of these experiences, our expectation of future authority figures is tainted and we continue to view them as destructive or abusive. Whether it involves husbands, bosses, or pastors, our present becomes a duplicate of our past experiences.

Based on this perspective, we can and do sabotage many relationships whether romantic, business, or personal. Our behavior patterns set others up to treat us the way we expect to be treated. Our reaction to others is in part based on our expectation of how they will treat us.

On the positive side of expectatations, there is the woman with the issue of blood in the fifth chapter of Mark.

> And a certain woman, which had an issue of blood twelve
> years, and had suffered many things of many physicians,
> and had spent all that she had, and was nothing bettered,
> but rather grew worse, when she had heard of Jesus, came in

the press behind, and touched his garment. For she said, If I may touch but his clothes, I shall be whole. And straightway the fountain of her blood was dried up; and she felt in her body that she was healed of that plague.

And Jesus, immediately knowing in himself that virtue had gone out of him, turned him about in the press, and said, Who touched my clothes? And his disciples said unto him, Thou seest the multitude thronging thee, and sayest thou, Who touched me? And he looked round about to see her that had done this thing. But the woman fearing and trembling, knowing what was done in her, came and fell down before him, and told him all the truth. And he said unto her, Daughter, thy faith hath made thee whole; go in peace, and be whole of thy plague. (Mark 5:25–34 KJV)

The woman had heard about the healing miracles of Jesus and developed the expectation that He could heal her if only she could touch the hem of His garment. Thus she sought to find Him and fulfill her expectation. Before she sought Him, she saw her healing in her mind. An image of this reality was already growing deep within her soul. After she touched Jesus, He asked, "Who touched me?" Her expectation drew from Him exactly what she had thought it would. Isn't that a powerful principle?

We draw from life as well as from others exactly what we expect.

If you grew up in a relatively normal home, you see things differently from a person who was raised in an abusive home. This person is less likely to allow abusive behavior in any relationship.

If your father figure was passive and nondemonstrative, you will be attracted to a mate with these personality qualities; if he had any kind of addiction, the chances of you marrying someone with the same problem increase exponentially.

Your first response may be, "That's absurd." I agree up to a point. You may believe addiction to be normal behavior for the authority figures in your life, and so this type of relationship feels normal or familiar. An expectation regarding the behaviors of men and woman and how they should relate to one another has developed deep within your soul.

Other factors could be involved. Maybe you still hold unforgiveness against your father figure for not giving you enough attention or not being there for you emotionally. This unforgiveness always remains well hidden deep within, and you may not be aware it exists. If this is the case, the law of reaping and sowing comes into play.

Each of us emanates a certain vibe about how we expect life to go. When we meet someone of the opposite sex and these vibes draw that person to us, the spiritual laws of reaping and sowing take effect.

If our father figure abused our mother emotionally, verbally, or physically, we can develop the expectation that all relationships will be abusive, that all men are abusive in one way or another, that all men are selfish and uncaring about our feelings.

Expectations are not as binding as a judgment or unforgiveness. Unforgiveness will always bring into play the law of reaping and sowing (Galatians 6:7) if left unresolved. Hidden judgments within our hearts create a breeding ground for us to duplicate the conduct for which we judged others (Romans 2:1). Expectation is less of an influence but will usually have an effect because we gravitate toward what we consider familiar.

Expectations proceed from the way we perceive life and the interactions of the authority figures around us. Our reality is a result of our interpretations of these experiences.

How do you see the world around you? Is your perception the whole truth or is it tainted by your life's experiences? Our expectations are indeed a result of things we have seen and experienced in the past. We are the sum total of our genetics, the environment in which we grew up, and all our experiences. This mix creates our characters and our personalities.

You do not have to remain who you are but can be all God has called you to be. The decision is entirely yours. What will you do with the information you have learned in this study? Will you tuck it away and say, "That was interesting," or will you press forward, applying the principles found in the Word of God and becoming all you can be in Christ?

Transformation into the image of Jesus is a process, a lifelong journey bought and paid for by the blood of Jesus. Our part in the process is to "study to show ourselves approved unto God, a workman that needeth not be ashamed, rightly dividing the word of truth" (2 Timothy 2:15 KJV).

God calls us to love others unconditionally just as He loves us. To love unconditionally means to move forward through an act of the will, regardless of what our emotions tell us. In other words, we must be obedient to the Word of God.

People who love conditionally react based on their emotions; their acceptance of us depends on what we do or don't do. If we displease them in any way, people who love conditionally always withdraw their love for a designated time, sometimes forever.

A person can withdraw emotionally without leaving physically. An emotional wound may be so severe that the person's spirit shuts down. This is usually what occurs in a rocky marriage. One partner hurts the other, and neither knows how to process the anger and the pain in a godly manner. The hurt festers and grows until the next time one of them hurts the other. The pain builds until the hurting person completely shuts himself or herself off emotionally from the other. This is the picture found in Hebrews 12:15.

"I beseech you therefore, brethren, by the mercies of God, that ye present your bodies a living sacrifice, holy, acceptable unto God, which is your reasonable service. And be not conformed to this world: but be ye transformed by the renewing of your mind, that ye may prove what is that good, and acceptable, and perfect, will of God" (Romans 12:1–2 KJV).

Reap in Kind (Newton's Third Law of Motion)

> Be not deceived; God is not mocked: for whatsoever a
> man soweth, that shall he also reap.
>
> —Galatians 6:7 KJV

Newton's third law holds that for every action there must be an equal and opposite reaction. If we harbor unforgiveness in our hearts against others who have wronged us, whether this hurt is imagined or real, we will continue to reap the same dysfunction in all our future relationships until we release forgiveness to these people. In praying to forgive another, we must also ask God to forgive us for judging. When we hold unforgiveness in our hearts toward others, we have set ourselves up as their judge.

The passage from Galatians says we will reap in our lives all that we have sown whether the sowing occurred in ignorance or with knowledge of what we were doing. Ignorance of our past wrongdoing does not negate God's spiritual laws. In future relationships, on the other hand, we can still reap good things.

Sin removes our free will in the area where the sin was committed, creating an involuntary reaction to a similar circumstance in the future as well as in the present.

Many people believe they have forgiven someone who has hurt them, but the fruits of unforgiveness remain in their lives for all to see. When we forgive others but do not ask God to forgive us for judging them, we complete only a portion of what He has called us to do to let go of an offense. If we do not repent for holding the offense against the person who has hurt us, we are not acting in obedience to God and the instructions He has left us in His Word.

God also calls us to pray for those who have hurt and offended us. "But I say unto you, Love your enemies, bless them that curse you, do good to them that hate you, and pray for them which despitefully use you, and persecute you" (Matthew 5:44 KJV).

People still harbor ill feelings or experience painful emotions about past wrongs because they have not obeyed this Scripture verse. Forgiveness is not complete until we not only forgive, but ask God to forgive us for holding others' sins against them. The next step is to duplicate Jesus' actions while He was on the cross and prayed, "Father, forgive them; for they know not what they do" (Luke 23:24).

When we are obedient to Matthew 5:44, God will begin not only to change our emotions concerning others, but to fill us with a God-given love for them.

Journey to Wholeness

Our problem is that we want a quick fix. We have a microwave mentality that demands instant results. Salvation is free, but wholeness in the emotional realm requires study, perseverance, self-denial, sacrifice, and daily obedience to the Word of God. Wholeness does not automatically come when we are born again.

"Who his own self bare our sins in his own body on the tree, that we, being dead to sins, should live unto righteousness: by whose stripes ye were healed" (1 Peter 2:24 KJV).

We are not automatically or instantly delivered from curses by Christ's death and resurrection until we appropriate God's promises in our lives.

All promises must be appropriated. To do this, we must recognize and apply spiritual principles. If we were automatically delivered from the curses of Deuteronomy 28:15 when we were born again, why do Christians get sick with cancer, diabetes, high blood pressure, mental illness, and addictions? Why do Christians fight the temptations of drugs, adultery, or other fleshly sin?

If deliverance from curses were automatic when we became born again, why do human beings still have to suffer physical death? Were not these problems all a result of the fall of Adam and Eve and their disobedience to God? Didn't the fall bring death and disease and force men to work by the sweat of their brows and women to bear children in pain? Didn't the fall cost us face-to-face communication with God?

If our new birth in Christ brings automatic deliverance, why are we not instantly perfect the way Adam and Eve were in the garden before the fall?

After we are born again, God gives every one of us a choice about how we will live. Will we live as overcomers or will we live defeated lives?

On this awesome journey, we begin to know who our Father is and to recognize that He will do what He said He would do. To know in the Word of God means to be aware of, to feel, to perceive, to be sure, to understand clearly what is in the heart of the person with whom you enjoy an intimate relationship. An intimate relationship is possible with someone of either sex. Intimacy does not always mean a sexual relationship.

Wholeness will cost you everything.

What will you do with the information you have learned in this study? Will you go your way, forget all about it, becoming a lukewarm Christian, or will you pursue God with a passion and become all you can be in Him?

God will hold us all accountable when we stand before Him on judgment day. He has given us His Son, who died for our sins, as well as His Word, which encourages us, sustains us, and guides us into all truth.

What will you do with His Son? Will you accept or reject Him?

"Now therefore, thus says the Lord of hosts, 'Consider your ways! You have sown much, but harvest little; you eat, but there is not enough to be satisfied; you drink, but there is not enough to become drunk; you put on clothing, but no one is warm enough; and he who earns, earns wages to put into a purse with holes.' Thus says the Lord of hosts, 'Consider your ways'" (Haggai 1:5–7).

Home Study Guide

This home study is not intended to make you relive painful memories. Rather the goal is to give you time to reflect after the teachings and to process those memories in a safe and godly manner. You must pray and release those hurts you have not adequately surrendered due to a lack of knowledge or perhaps even with the knowledge that they are still affecting you.

Maybe you have hidden the memories because they were too painful to bear. All of us have done this. It is human nature. But remember that if feelings have not been experienced, expressed, or released, these memories lodge within your soul realm and hover there until they are called forth to serve your present circumstances. Surface they will and with vengeance! Remember that sin is progressive.

In the notes section you will find prayers that pertain to each situation you remember after a session. These have been provided for your journal entries.

1) Spiritual Laws vs. Natural Laws.

> ✗ Were you aware of the parallel between spiritual laws and natural laws before this class began?
> ✗ Can you think of any laws in the Word of God that parallel each other?
> ✗ Can you remember a time in your life when God overruled natural laws concerning something you needed?

> List those you can in the notes section in the back of this study guide. If you cannot think of any now, you will as the class progresses. You can list them at that time. Also, remember that God's supernatural laws supersede any natural laws. He is sovereign and can do as He chooses.

Turn to your notes section and journal these events.

2) Conception with Adamic Nature.

3) Genesis 2:16–17; Genesis 3:6–7.

    ✘ Can you think of a time/times in your life when wrong choices created difficult circumstances for you?

    ✘ Has God already turned these wrong choices around for you, or are you still waiting for your miracle?

There may be an unprocessed root in your childhood if you are still experiencing any of these circumstances. Ask God to show you the roots as we study His Word together. If you would like to make a list, you can do so in your notes section. Listing these may help you to acknowledge them, bringing them to the surface for healing as you recognize their existence and learn appropriate ways of processing them.

4) Action of an Authority Figure (childhood memories).

5) Deuteronomy 5:16; Ephesians 4:26–27; Proverbs 3:1–6; Hebrews 12:15; Mark 11:22–26; Matthew 5:44; Galatians 6:7.

    ✘ Can you remember any instances where you felt verbally, physically, or sexually abused?

    ✘ Was one or both of your parents/authority figures alcoholic, drug-addicted, or workaholic?

    ✘ Did one or both of your parents/authority figures favor a sibling over you?

    ✘ Did you feel neglected, abandoned, or rejected?

    ✘ Did any other abuse occur?

    ✘ Did you receive love and affirmation as a child?

    ✘ Did your parents' divorce? Did one of them die, abandon, or reject you?

- ✗ Was one of your parents unfaithful?
- ✗ Were you conceived out of wedlock?

If you feel pain regarding any of the above memories, turn to the prayer guide in the back of this study concerning anger, unforgiveness, or bitterness. It also might help to journal these feelings in the notes section when praying.

6) How to Honor Authority.

7) Matthew 5:44–48; Titus 3:1–6.

- ✗ Can you remember times when you dishonored authority figures?
- ✗ Were you rebellious growing up?
- ✗ If your parents/authority figures are still alive, have you asked them to forgive you?
- ✗ Have you asked God for forgiveness for these sinful actions?
- ✗ Have you processed them according to the Word of God?

If you are just now realizing that you dishonored authority figures in the past, it's not too late to make things right with God and perhaps with the people you dishonored if they are still alive.

If you were rebellious as a child or a teenager, hidden deep within your spirit and soul is the pain of rejection. Begin to journal these feelings, then go to the "Prayers for Deliverance" section and process these memories.

As the Holy Spirit brings back other memories, list each in your prayer journal. Find "Prayer for Forgiveness for Dishonoring Authority Figures" and pray it. Also, do not forget to forgive yourself as well for being less than perfect due to your lack of knowledge. It is not too late.

8) Perception.

> ✗ Can you identify areas where you received wrong perceptions due to the home in which you grew up?
> ✗ Did you receive a distorted view of the opposite sex because of your parents' views or because of an offense by one parent against another?

Ask God to show you any perceptions contrary to His will that lie hidden within your soul realm. List anything the Holy Spirit brings to your remembrance in your notes section. Go straight to the prayer section to process these memories one by one.

9) Anger.

10) Ephesians 4:26–27; Proverbs 3:1–2.

> ✗ Can you remember any time when you were especially angry as a child?
> ✗ Do you still feel angry over a particular incident in your childhood?
> ✗ Do you feel that you've forgiven your authority figures for past injustices but still feel anger when you think or speak of certain occasions?
> ✗ Are you still carrying anger or emotional pain regarding hurts inflicted on you by relatives, mates, friends, or business associates?
> ✗ Do you get angry easily when things do not go your way?
> ✗ Do you get angry when someone does not agree with you?
> ✗ Are you using anger to control others?

Journal in your notes anything you remember regarding emotions that keep surfacing from your past; go to your prayer section and pray the prayer concerning anger for each item, one by one, plucking up the seeds of anger, unforgiveness, bitterness, and judgment.

11) Bitterness.

12) Hebrews 12:15.

> ✗ Do you still feel bitterness concerning something or someone in your past?
> ✗ Do you say, "If such and such had not happened to me, I would not be in this predicament today"?
> ✗ Have you allowed any unforgiveness to fester like a sore for years without resolving it?

Journal in your notes those things you remember, and pray from the prayer examples regarding anything that still bothers you.

13) Unforgiveness.

14) Mark 11:22–26; Matthew 6:14–15; Matthew 5:12–13; Luke 23:33–34; Matthew 43–48; Luke 6:27–28.

> ✗ Can you think of anyone you have not forgiven?
> ✗ Do you say you have forgiven, but continue to experience painful emotions when you remember the incident?
> ✗ Can you remember any hurtful incidents from the past that you have not processed in a godly way?
> ✗ Are you still rehashing old memories?

True forgiveness has not occurred in your heart if you answered yes to any of these questions.

God requires us to forgive others. Journal these feelings, then go to the "Prayer for Deliverance" section and process these memories one by one.

15) Reap in Kind.

16) Galatians 6:7

> ✗ Can you think of any type of situation that keeps repeating itself in your life?
> ✗ Can you see repetitive dysfunctional behavioral patterns in your relationships?
> ✗ Is there any type of behavior you dislike/despise in your mate that you recognize was in a prior mate or perhaps even a parent?

There may be remains of an undetected root of unforgiveness deep within your soul that began in your childhood and must be processed. Have you remembered similar behaviors in one or both of your parents? If so, there were circumstances in your childhood that created pain in this particular area. Again, go to the prayer section of this study guide and pray the forgiveness prayer concerning each pattern you remember.

17) Judgments.

18) Romans 2:1; Matthew 7:1–5.

> ✗ Can you remember a time/times when you judged someone for something and ended up doing the very same thing?
> ✗ Can you remember commenting about how wrong a person was for doing something, then finding yourself in the same kind of circumstance?

If God brings something to your memory, go to the prayer section on judgments and begin to journal and to pray.

19) Journey to Wholeness.

> ✗ Are you ready to stop blaming others for your circumstances in life?
> ✗ Are you ready to take responsibility for your actions, allowing others to make their own choices without trying to coerce and manipulate them for your own benefit?

> If you answered yes, go to the "Morning Prayer of Consecration" and rededicate yourself to the plan God has for your life. Journaling this prayer and your thoughts would help. Remember that the prayer of consecration is a daily prayer intended to open yourself to God's power and allow Him to change you into His image.

20) Inner Vows.

21) Matthew 5:34–37.

> ✗ Can you remember any inner vows you made, either silently or verbally, while experiencing emotional or physical pain? In times of emotional pain, did you say, "I'll never let anyone hurt me again"?
> ✗ Are there issues in your life that seem to have a persistent grip on you or that you don't understand?

> Ask God to show you any hidden inner vows you may have made of which you not aware. Then go to the "Prayer Concerning Inner Vows" in the prayer section, journaling, praying, and processing each vow individually as God brings it to your memory.

22) Heart of Stone.

23) Ezekiel 36:25; Psalm 51:10.

- ✗ What were your authority figure/figures like?
- ✗ Did they hold you, cuddle you, and give you affection?
- ✗ Do you feel hard or uncaring in any area of your life?
- ✗ Have you been hurt so badly that you now say, "I just don't care anymore"?

Journal your thoughts in the prayer section and then ask God to show you any areas where you still have a heart of stone.

24) Wounded/Slumbering Spirit.

25) Proverbs 18:14; Proverbs 17:22; Romans 13:11.

My spirit experienced emotional wounding each time I was offended and allowed the transgression to remain unprocessed in a godly fashion. These wounds stunted the growth of my spirit, rendering it incapable of responding to others in an adult and godly fashion.

Ask God to show you any areas of your spirit that remain immature and in need of His illuminating light. Journal the things He shows you in your notes section.

26) Expectations.

27) Galatians 6:7.

Women, have you ever heard your mother or authority figure say, "Men are all alike"? Have you ever said this or any of the things below?

- ✗ Men want only one thing.
- ✗ A man will use you, then throw you away.
- ✗ Men cannot be trusted.
- ✗ All men are self-centered.

✗ Men cannot be trusted with finances because they will spend money selfishly.

✗ Do not ever let a man know who you really are inside because he will only hurt you by using the information against you.

Men, have you ever heard your father or another male authority figures say, "Women are all alike"? Have you ever said this or any of the things below?

✗ Women want you only for your money.

✗ Women will only use you, then go their own way.

✗ Women cannot be trusted.

✗ All women are self-centered.

✗ Women cannot be trusted with finances because they will spend money selfishly.

✗ Do not ever let a woman know who you really are inside because she will only hurt you by using the information against you.

Were any of these statements made in the home where you grew up? Have you or someone close to you voiced the same negative sentiments? Maybe the statements were not made openly, but the message was relayed to you nonetheless. If so, perhaps hidden deep within is an unhealthy expectation regarding men or women, or some other negative outlook you may not even know exists.

Hidden expectations residing deep within your soul may have allowed the development of sabotaging behavior patterns without your ever realizing it.

Ask God to show you any hidden expectations deep within you that have caused trouble in your life.

"Search me, O God, and know my heart; try me and know my anxious thoughts; and see if there be any hurtful way in me, and lead me in the everlasting way" (Psalm 139:23-24 NASB).

When I Change

When I change my thinking, I change my beliefs.

When I change my beliefs, I change my expectations.

When I change my expectations, I change my attitude.

When I change my attitude, I change my behavior.

When I change my behavior, I change my performance.

When I change my performance, I change
my life and truly impact others!

—Author Unknown

Morning Prayer of Consecration

Father, I come to You in the name of Jesus. I believe that Jesus died on the cross for my sins and that You are the truth, the light, and the way; there is no other. I believe Jesus died on the cross for my sins and rose again from the dead.

I give You my wrong mind-sets, strongholds, patterns of thinking, motives, and attitudes. I give You my will and pray not my will but Yours be done.

I submit myself to You spirit, soul, and body and give myself to You as a willing living sacrifice. Use me for Your glory any way You choose. Thy kingdom come, Thy will be done in my life.

I give up all my rebellion and independence, my pride and self-centeredness, my harboring of rejection and inferiority, and my bitterness and unforgiveness. I give up all my sin and submit myself to You.

I confess all my sins before You and ask for Your forgiveness. Release me now from the power of the enemy of my soul. Because You paid the price for my sins, I forgive myself for all the wrongs of the past, and I accept myself.

In the name of Jesus Christ, I pull down every stronghold and renounce the power of Satan in my life. By faith, I now receive my release, and I thank You, Lord, for setting me free! Amen.

Prayers for Deliverance

Confess out loud the following prayers as needed.

Prayer for Forgiveness for Dishonoring Authority Figures

Father, I come to You in the name of Jesus. I ask You to forgive me for judging and holding unforgiveness against my (parent/parents, authority figures; name each one). Wash me in Your blood and release me from this curse. I wash every negative word I have spoken against them with the blood of Jesus, canceling the effect upon my life and theirs (if they are still alive).

I release forgiveness to my (parent/parents, authority figures; name each one) for (name the incidents) and ask You not to hold this sin to their charge, because they did not know what they were doing. (If they are still alive, pray blessings upon them.)

I ask You to bless them with Your truth, to send laborers across their path with the gospel of truth (if they are unsaved), and to open their eyes to see the height and the depth of Your love for them.

I bind every demonic force associated with this curse, commanding it to depart and to leave me and my family immediately. I embrace Your mercy and grace concerning this situation in the name of Jesus.

Father, I ask You to minister to the hurting child within me. Heal my painful memories and bring total restoration to my spirit, soul, and body. I wash my soul and every memory hidden in my subconscious with Your precious blood and declare myself clean.

Prayer to Forgive Others

Father, I come to You in the name of Jesus. Because You have forgiven me for my sins, I make the conscience choice to forgive (name person/

81

persons) for (name incident/incidents you are releasing). I ask You to forgive me for judging them and for holding the offense against them in my heart.

I ask You not to hold this sin against them, because they did not know what they were doing.

I ask You to bless them with Your truth, to send laborers across their path with the gospel of truth (if they are unsaved), and to open their eyes to see the height and the depth of Your love for them.

Father, I ask You to minister to the hurting child within me. Heal my painful memories and bring total restoration to my spirit, soul, and body. I wash my soul and my spirit as well as every memory hidden in my subconscious with Your precious blood and declare myself clean.

I ask You to create in me a heart of flesh and to remove the heart of stone and the walls I have erected trying to protect myself from pain. I surrender my all to You in the name of Jesus.

Prayer to Forgive Yourself

Father, I come to You in the name of Jesus. By an act of my free will, I choose to forgive myself for _____ (say out loud that which holds you captive). You've forgiven me and placed my sins under the blood. Therefore I release forgiveness to myself as well, never again to be tormented by Satan for my past deeds.

Satan, I bind and release you from myself by the blood and the name of Jesus, commanding you to cease tormenting me concerning this matter. I wash my memories in the blood of Jesus and declare that I am a blood-washed child of the Most High God and that I stand in His righteousness!

Prayer for Judgments Made Against Others

Father, I come to You in the name of Your Son, Jesus. I ask You to forgive me for judging (name the person/persons) for (name the incident/incidents for which you have judged them whether in your heart or out loud to someone). They are Your servants, and I do not know what You have called them to do. Therefore I repent of becoming their judge in this matter. I bring to the cross of Calvary this judgment, rendering it null and void and washing it in the Blood of Jesus. I ask You to bless them and to give them Your wisdom in every area of their lives.

(Continue to pray blessings upon them as God leads you.)

Prayer Concerning Inner Vows

Father, I come to You in the name of Your Son, Jesus. I ask Your forgiveness for the inner vow (name the vow whether it was made in your heart or out loud) I made against (name the person/persons or yourself). I ask You to release me from the bondage and the dysfunction that this vow has brought into my life.

In the name of Jesus and by the power of His blood, I now renounce, break, and nullify this vow and confess that I am released from the hold it has had on me. I command any evil spirits that have taken advantage of this unholy vow to leave me now in the name of Jesus!

(Next, confess over yourself the promises of the Word of God concerning your situation. Repeat this prayer for every inner vow God brings to your memory.)

Prayer Concerning a Wounded/Slumbering Spirit

Father, I ask You to heal the painful memories of my past, release me from these strongholds, wash my spirit in Your blood, and set me free. I sever by the blood of Jesus the old dysfunctional pathways in my brain, and I ask You to recreate new Christ-like pathways for relating to others. I sever by the blood of Jesus all communication, supply, and power lines between myself and Satan's evil forces.

I speak confusion to the enemy camp concerning its assignment against me.

"No weapon that is formed against me shall prosper; and every tongue that shall rise against me in judgment I shall condemn. This is the heritage of the servants of the Lord, and their righteousness is of me, saith the Lord" (Isaiah 54:17 KJV). [Use of the first person is mine.]

I declare that I am a blood-washed child of the Most High God, the King of the universe, standing in the righteousness of Christ my Lord and King!

Prayer Concerning Expectations

Father, I come to You in the name of Jesus. I ask Your forgiveness for the wrong expectations concerning (name the specific expectation God showed you) that I developed in my past.

I bind you, Satan, and all your demonic forces, commanding you to depart from me in the name of Jesus.

Father, I ask You to end my old ways of thinking and to create new patterns of thinking in me concerning this matter. I thank You for the blood of Jesus that sets me free not only in this area, but in every area of my life.

I ask You, Holy Spirit, to remind me when these old patterns try to resurface and to help me make right choices regarding this area of my life in the future.

(Pray in the spirit as the Holy Ghost leads you.)

Prayer for Salvation

> There is salvation in no one else, for there is no other name under heaven given among mortals by which we must be saved.
>
> —Acts 4:12 NRSV

> That if thou shalt confess with thy mouth the Lord Jesus, and shalt believe in thine heart that God hath raised him from the dead, thou shalt be saved. For with the heart man believeth unto righteousness; and with the mouth confession is made unto salvation.
>
> —Romans 10:9–10 KJV

Father, I come to You in the name of Jesus, knowing I am a sinner. I believe that Jesus died on the cross for my sins, rising on the third day. You are the truth, the light, and the way, and there is no other.

I confess all my sins before You and ask Your forgiveness. Release me now from the power of the enemy of my soul and set me free.

I give You my wrong mind-sets, strongholds, patterns of thinking, motives, and attitudes. I give You my will and pray not my will but Yours be done. I give my life to You to use any way You wish.

I receive You as my savior, in the name of Jesus. Amen.

Notes

Notes

Healing Gestational Wounds

Part 3

> The wicked are estranged from the womb: they go
> astray as soon as they be born, speaking lies.
> —Psalm 58:3 KJV

"Yea, thou heardest not; yea, thou knewest not; yea, from that time that thine ear was not opened: for I knew that thou wouldest deal very treacherously, and wast <u>called a transgressor from the womb</u>" (Isaiah 48:8 KJV). [Emphasis mine]

In this verse, God was chastising His people Israel for their unfaithfulness, their rebellion, and their idol worship. He was speaking to us as well since we are the adopted children of God.

Through his or her spirit, a baby in the womb understands far more than we thought in the past he or she could know. The baby is able to experience what occurs in the home. He or she can react or sin in the spirit against his or her environment, respond to outside stimuli such as music, learn from Mom or Dad's voice whether they are getting along or having a conflict, and determine numerous other outside conditions. The baby also takes as his or her own the emotions the mother feels while she is pregnant.

"Behold, I was shapen in iniquity; and in sin did my mother conceive me. Behold, thou desirest truth in the inward parts: and in the hidden part thou shalt make me to know wisdom" (Psalm 51:5–6 KJV).

King David spoke these words after Nathan the priest confronted him about his adulteress sin with Bathsheba and the resulting murder of her husband Uriah (2 Samuel 11). He was acknowledging his conception and how a sinful nature was imparted to him in the process. He said that his mother conceived him with this nature to do wrong instead of right. Yet he admitted that God desires us all to pursue divine truth in our spirit and therefore know wisdom.

A Baby in the Womb Aware of His Surroundings

> And Mary arose in those days, and went into the hill country with haste, into a city of Juda; and entered into the house of Zacharias, and saluted Elisabeth. And it came to pass, that, when Elisabeth heard the salutation of Mary, the babe leaped in her womb; and Elisabeth was filled with the Holy Ghost: And she spake out with a loud voice, and said, Blessed art thou among women, and blessed is the fruit of thy womb. And whence is this to me, that the mother of my Lord should come to me? For, lo, as soon as the voice of thy salutation sounded in mine ears, the babe leaped in my womb for joy.
>
> —Luke 1:39–44 KJV

When Mary was pregnant with Jesus, she went to her cousin Elisabeth's house. Elisabeth was approximately six months' pregnant with John the Baptist. We see that John leaped in Elisabeth's womb. This was because he heard Mary's voice and knew Mary was carrying his Savior, Jesus. From this passage, we can see that John's spirit was alert and sensitive to his surroundings and had the capacity to recognize Jesus and to respond with joy.

You may ask how an undeveloped baby inside its mother's womb could possibly be aware of its surroundings.

All life emanates from our Father God. Without Him, life could not exist. When God breathed into Adam's lifeless body a portion of His own spirit, Adam became a living soul capable of sustaining life. God breathed this part of Himself into Adam and gave life to the human form that He created from the dust of the ground. God's spirit enters all human beings at conception and gives them the capability of knowing what is transpiring in their surroundings.

"And the Lord God formed man of the dust of the ground, and breathed into his nostrils the breath of life; and man became a living soul" (Genesis 2:7 KJV).

Jewish Culture

In Jewish culture, pregnant women resigned from all physical responsibilities and stayed with a relative for the first three to five months of a pregnancy. During this time, the woman meditated, prayed, sang spiritual songs, and read aloud from the Scriptures. Jews believe that in the first three to five months of pregnancy the character and the personality of the unborn infant are developed.

"But there is a spirit in man: and the inspiration of the Almighty giveth them understanding" (Job 32:8 KJV).

Our spirits have understanding that comes to us from God the Father. Even in the womb when the fleshly brain has not fully developed, the spirit of the fetus is already aware of what is going on around it.

Jacob and Esau

> And Isaac entreated the Lord for his wife, because she was barren: and the Lord was entreated of him, and Rebekah his wife conceived. And the children struggled together within her; and she said, If it be so, why am I thus? And she went to inquire of the Lord. And the Lord said unto her, Two nations are in thy womb, and two manner of people shall be separated from thy bowels; and the one people shall be stronger than the other people; and the elder shall serve the younger.
> —Genesis 25:21–23 KJV

This passage tells us that there was a struggle going on between Esau and Jacob while they were still in the womb. How could this possibly occur if their spirits were not aware and were unable to experience jealously? How could they possibly have known in the womb that each of them would father a nation?

When we were conceived in our mothers' wombs, God placed DNA into our spirits, having known us before the foundation of the world. With our free will, we determine our own destinies. He does not force us to obey His Word or to follow His will for our lives. When we choose our own will and stray from His plan, we get into trouble, casting aside the shield of faith and allowing Satan to enter our lives.

Predestined before the Foundation of the World

> According as he hath chosen us in him before the foundation of the world, that we should be holy and without blame before him in love: Having predestinated us unto the adoption of children by Jesus Christ to himself, according to the good pleasure of his will, to the praise of the glory of his grace, wherein he hath made us accepted in the beloved. In whom we have redemption through his blood, the forgiveness of sins, according to the riches of his grace; wherein he hath abounded toward us in all wisdom and prudence; having made known unto us the mystery of his will, according to his good pleasure which he hath purposed in himself: That in the dispensation of the fullness of times he might gather together in one all things in Christ, both which are in heaven, and which are on earth; even in him: In whom also we have obtained an inheritance, being predestinated according to the purpose of him who worketh all things after the counsel of his own will: That we should be to the praise of his glory, who first trusted in Christ.
>
> —Ephesians 1:4–12 KJV

Experiences of the Unborn

Among other things, our spirits experience distress, envy, faithfulness or unfaithfulness, fear, worship, and praise.

People can feel rejection even from conception, thus clouding their perceptions of life. Unborn babies know if they were planned or unwanted, conceived in adultery, incest, or out of wedlock. They know through their spirits, not their minds. Doctors have reported that newborn babies will sometimes not nurse from their mothers. After studying numerous cases of babies who rejected their mothers at birth, researchers found that in many instances the mothers or perhaps both the mother and the father had not planned the child's conception or birth. Perhaps the mother and the father were not married, or perhaps they were married but had not intended the pregnancy. The child was rejected; thus the child rejected the parent by not nursing.

Conditions That Can Affect the Unborn Child

In *Prenatal Wounds and Sins*, John and Paula Sandford detail some of the traits that children and parents in dysfunctional situations may develop.

1) An unwanted child will have a performance orientation, striving to earn the right to be. He may have an inordinate desire to please (or the opposite, rejecting others before he can be rejected. He may often apologize, suffer tension and frequent illness, have problems with bonding, refuse affection (or have an insatiable desire for it), and wish for death.
2) A child born out of wedlock may have a deep sense of shame and lack a sense of belonging.
3) A child born at a bad time financially may believe he is a burden.
4) A child born to parents too young may believe he is an intrusion.

5) A child born to a mother who suffers poor health may feel guilty for being; the child may take emotional responsibility for the mother.

6) A child whom one or both parents consider to be the wrong sex may suffer sexual identification problems; this is sometimes a cause of homosexuality. The child may strive to please, to be what the parents want, feel futility, and have a defeatist attitude ("I was wrong from the beginning"). A child trying to be the sex the parents wanted could become an effeminate boy or a tomboyish girl.

7) A child who follows conceptions that were lost may be overserious and overachieving, striving to make up for the loss. The child may be angry at being a "replacement" and not getting to be "me."

8) There may be fighting in the home.

9) A child may be nervous, uptight, and fearful. He may jump in to control a discussion when differences of opinion emerge, feeling guilty ("I'm the reason for this quarrel"). The child may take emotional responsibility for the parents.

10) The father may die or leave.

11) The child may suffer guilt, self-blame, anger, and the expectation of being abandoned. He may suffer depression and have a death wish.

12) The mother may lose a loved one and be consumed by grief.

13) The child may suffer loneliness, deep sadness, or depression, have a death wish or a fear of death. He may decide, "There is no support for me; I will have to depend on myself."

14) The couple will have unwholesome sexual relations. The father's approaches to the mother may be insensitive or violent, or he may have more than one sexual partner.

15) The mother or the father may have an aversion to sex or a generally unhealthy attitude regarding it.

16) Mother may be afraid of gaining too much weight and not eat properly.

17) The mother may have an insatiable hunger and be angry.

18) The child may be given away for adoption.

19) The child may always feel rejection or have an identity crisis.

Solution

Jesus never made a mistake nor will He ever make one. You were not a mistake, but were planned by God before the foundation of the world. Before the world existed, He knew the provision His Son would make by dying for our sins and restoring the relationship between Himself and all humanity.

"For thou hast possessed my reins: thou hast covered me in my mother's womb. I will praise thee; for I am fearfully and wonderfully made: marvelous are thy works; and that my soul knoweth right well" (Psalm 139:13–14).

True freedom from our past comes by diligently seeking God's will for our lives. He says, "And ye shall seek me, and find me, when ye shall search for me with all your heart" (Jeremiah 29:13 KJV).

"Call unto me, and I will answer thee, and shew thee great and mighty things, which thou knowest not" (Jeremiah 33:3 KJV).

If you recognize any of the character traits mentioned above in yourself, do not be discouraged. It is not too late for you. Deep in your spirit while you were in the womb, you got angry with your parents for not wanting you, for fighting, or for other reasons. Forgiveness is between God and you. Your parent, parents, authority figure or figures do not have to be alive for the forgiveness to work. You can forgive your parents even if one or both of them are deceased. Release forgiveness to your parents and ask God to forgive you for judging them.

Home Study Guide

Psalm 58:3; Isaiah 48:8; Psalm 51:5-6; Luke 1:39-44; Genesis 2:7; Job 32:8; Genesis 25:21-23; Ephesians 1:4-12; Psalm 139:13-14; Jeremiah 33:3.

- ✗ Has one or both of your parents ever told you that you were not planned or that you were a mistake?
- ✗ Were you conceived out of wedlock?
- ✗ Was your conception the result of rape or incest?
- ✗ Has your parent or parents ever told you that your conception came at a bad time financially?
- ✗ Did your parents separate or divorce while you were still in the womb?
- ✗ Were you adopted?

If you answered yes to any of these questions and have not processed these emotional issues in a godly fashion, rest assured they remain. These unprocessed emotions are subconsciously directing and affecting every aspect of your life whether or not you are aware of them.

Be completely honest with yourself, asking the Holy Spirit to reveal any hidden areas that you have repressed all your life. Wholeness cannot come unless honesty is paramount. Stir yourself, get alone with God, and do some much-needed homework in this area.

Begin to journal your feelings and pray the prayer for deliverance that follows in the next section.

"Create in me a clean heart, O God; and renew a right spirit within me" (Psalm 51:10 KJV).

Prayer for Deliverance

Father, I come to You in the name of Your, Son Jesus. You made me with a will of my own so I could freely make choices in my life. Because of Your great love, You sent Your Son to die on the cross of Calvary so that I might have my sins forgiven and enjoy the abundant life You so freely paid for. I make a conscious choice to forgive my parents for _____ (not wanting me when I was conceived, for wanting a child of a different sex; fill in the blank concerning your situation). I ask You to forgive me for judging them in this situation and for holding this against them all these years.

(If they are still alive) I ask You not to hold their sins against them, because they did not know what they were doing. Send laborers across their paths to bring them Your truth. Open their eyes so they can understand Your infinite love for them, which began before the foundation of the world. Father, I ask You to bless them.

Father, I loose wrong mind-sets and strongholds that have controlled me in the past and ask You to create in me the mind of Christ in these areas so that I can become all that You have called me to be. I bind my feet to Your pathway so that I may walk pleasing in Your sight. I bind my mind and my thought patterns to Your mind so that my thoughts are pleasing to You. I bind my will to Your will so that I may please You in every way.

I ask You to wash my soul with your precious blood, cleansing me from all the painful emotions that have built up within me all these years. Hold the hurting little girl or boy within and walk with me into maturity in this area of my soul and my spirit. Amen.

(If you will forgive your parents for being less than perfect and ask God to forgive you for judging them, He will release you from those patterns of behavior that have brought you so much pain in the past.)

Notes

Notes

Soul Ties

Part 4

Soul ties are a knitting together or bonding of two souls for blessing or for tremendous destruction if the tie is not of a godly nature.

Spirit

The spirit is the breath of life, which gives us God consciousness, allowing communication with the Most High.

"But there is a spirit in man; and the inspiration of the Almighty giveth them understanding" (Job 32:8 KJV).

Soul

The soul is the mind, the will, the emotions, the intellect, and self-consciousness (imagination, conscience, memory, reason, and affections).

"Why art thou cast down, O my soul? And why art thou disquieted in me? Hope thou in God; for I shall yet praise him for the help of his countenance. O my God, my soul is cast down within me. Therefore will I remember thee from the land of Jordan, and of the Hermonites, from the hill Mizar" (Psalm 42:5–6 KJV)

Body

The body is the seat of the senses (sight, hearing, smell, taste, and touch), the means by which the spirit and the soul have world consciousness.

"Now this I say, brethren, that flesh and blood cannot inherit the kingdom of God; neither doth corruption inherit incorruption" (1 Corinthians 15:50 KJV).

Godly Soul Ties

"Two are better than one; because they have a good reward for their labour. For if they fall, the one will lift up his fellow: but woe to him that is alone when he falleth; for he hath not another to help him up. Again, if two lie together, then they have heat: but how can one be warm alone? And if one prevail against him, two shall withstand him; and a threefold cord is not quickly broken" (Ecclesiastics 4:9–12 KJV).

In the Old Testament, David and Jonathan provide a good example of godly soul ties

"And it came to pass, when he had made an end of speaking unto Saul, that the soul of Jonathan was knit with the soul of David, and Jonathan loved him as his own soul" (1 Samuel 18:1 KJV).

The two became one in the soul realm. Jonathan was the rightful heir to the throne of his father Saul. Because of the soul tie, Jonathan was willing to give up his right to inherit the throne in favor of his best friend, David, whom God had anointed to be king in his stead. This was love in its purest, most unselfish form.

Ruth and her mother-in-law Naomi offer another example.

"And Ruth said, Entreat me not to leave thee, or to return from following after thee: for whither thou goest, I will go; and where thou lodgest, I will lodge: thy people shall be my people, and thy God my God" (Ruth 1:16 KJV).

Another example of godly soul ties comes from the New Testament.

"And the multitude of them that believed were of one heart and of one soul: neither said any of them that ought of the things which he possessed was his own; but they had all things common" (Acts 4:32 KJV).

God intends the body of Christ to be one in spirit and in soul.

Parent-and-Child Soul Ties

When a child is born, a soul tie should develop between the parents and the baby. This tie is healthy and provides love, security, and stability to the child.

However, if the soul tie with one child is greater than the tie with another child, if the parent favors one child to the detriment of another, this unnatural tie will disrupt the whole household.

Consider Isaac and Rebekah in Genesis 27. Isaac loved Esau over Jacob, and Rebekah loved Jacob over Esau. Look at the destruction the curse of favoritism, perpetuated into the next generation, created in this family.

Another unnatural soul tie existed between Jacob and his son Joseph. "Now Israel loved Joseph more than all his children, because he was the son of his old age: and he made him a coat of many colors" (Genesis 37:3 KJV).

An unnatural soul tie brought destruction to this family. This was a dysfunctional household. The favoritism his father showed him created character flaws in Joseph and fractured the relationship between him and his siblings. Because of his steadfast obedience to God, Joseph's situation eventually worked out for the best. God used these circumstances to purge him and to make him ready for service to the Most High.

Out of jealousy, Joseph's brothers sold him to the Ishmeelites, and he soon found himself a slave to Potiphar. "And the Midianites sold him into Egypt unto Potiphar, an officer of Pharaoh's, and captain of the guard" (Genesis 37:36 KJV).

Sometimes we do not always realize the effect our behaviors and emotional needs are having on others. That is why I have included the morning prayer of consecration in this study guide. I hope it will become a part of your prayer life, always keeping you open to God's will for your life.

Generational Curses/Soul Ties

Addictions are an example of generational curses that exist in families. The soul ties that addictions create must be broken if the addicted person is to be free. Soul ties and generational curses become entwined, and each must be broken to free all family members involved.

In part 2 of this study guide, "Spiritual Laws and Cycles," I mentioned unforgiveness and judgments made against parents or authority figures concerning painful incidents that occurred in your past. These unprocessed sins are the open door for addiction and generational curses to continue in your life. The only way to stop the addiction is to break the curse, then process the memories, using the prayers for deliverance in that section.

Perfect Soul Tie: Marriage

> And Adam said, This is now bone of my bones, and flesh of
> my flesh: she shall be called Woman, because she was taken out
> of Man. Therefore shall a man leave his father and his mother,
> and shall cleave unto his wife: and they shall be one flesh.
> —Genesis 2:22–23 KJV

The phrase *one flesh* also appears in Matthew 19:4–6 and Mark 10:7–9. God's purpose for husband and wife is that they be one in spirit, soul, and flesh, that they enjoy unity.

If a person is sharing with a member of the opposite sex things that should be first shared with a spouse, this is an emotional affair and it is sin!

You should not be complaining about your spouse to a person of the opposite sex. If you have an issue regarding your spouse, share it with a prayer partner, who can objectively counsel and pray with you. You must not complain to anyone who is willing to listen to your grievances concerning your relationship. This is an open door for Satan to gain entrance into your marriage. By giving to another what God intended for your spouse, you are fragmenting your emotional relationship with your spouse and wasting the energy required to work out your problems. There are no excuses!

Your spouse should be the first to know what is going on inside of you and any decisions you have made or are contemplating concerning things that are important to both of you.

> *Your spouse's feelings should be your first concern in any decision you make whether it is about finances, emotional, physical, or spiritual matters.*

Both of you, not just one of you, should make all decisions concerning your finances and other important areas of your lives. A couple should make no large purchases until husband and wife are in total agreement. This is of vital importance to the health and well-being of a relationship.

"Giving thanks always for all things unto God and the Father in the name of our Lord Jesus Christ; <u>submitting yourselves one to another</u> in the fear of God" (Ephesians 5:20–21 KJV). [Emphasis mine]

Do not let your spouse hear from someone else something you should have shared with him or her first. This is tremendously damaging to your relationship. It will drive an emotional wedge between you and could eventually destroy your marriage. Each spouse needs to know deep down inside his or her importance to the other.

If you are sharing with someone else feelings, facts, problems, dreams for the future, or other things that should be shared with your spouse first, you need to seek God with fasting and prayer to find out why you do not trust your spouse with who you are deep down inside. You must ask God to reveal the basis for the fear that remains hidden deep within you.

You may ask why I refer to fear in this situation. If you did not have a spirit of fear, you would share with your spouse every area of your life. Deep inside you are afraid that if your spouse knew everything about you, he or she would condemn you and use your secrets against you in some way.

On the other hand, you may have festering unresolved grievances that you have not released or processed in a righteous and godly manner. These grievances may be the result of little annoyances or hurts of which your spouse may not be aware. If you want your marriage or any other relationship to be all God called it to be, if you want to fulfill God's destiny for your life, you must forgive and let the past become the past. Please refer to the prayer for deliverance in part 2.

Destructive Sexual Soul Ties

> Know ye not that your bodies are the members of Christ? shall I then take the members of Christ, and make them the members of an harlot? God forbid. What? know ye not that he which is joined to an harlot is one body? for two, saith he, shall be one flesh. But he that is joined unto the Lord is one spirit. Flee fornication. Every sin that a man doeth is without the body; but he that committeth

fornication sinneth against his own body. What? know ye
not that your body is the temple of the Holy Ghost which is
in you, which ye have of God, and ye are not your own? For
ye are bought with a price: therefore glorify God in your
body, and in your spirit, which are God's.

—1 Corinthians 6:15–20 KJV

Sexual intercourse outside of the marriage creates an unhealthy soul
tie that is a sin against one's own body. Notice the Word says that they
become one flesh even though they are not married. Regardless of
their matrimonial status, this is what happens when two people are
sexually intimate.

This sinful soul tie makes a person unable to commit to one partner.
That's because each time the person has sex, he or she is leaving a
part of himself or herself behind with a different partner. Such people
are also taking into their souls a portion of the person or persons
with whom they have become intimate, resulting in fragmentation
of the soul realm. Ignorant of this biblical truth, we enter into sexual
relationships and even marriage when we are less than whole and
therefore unable to present our total selves to one another in the way
God intended.

During intercourse, a portion of the person's soul and spirit transfers
into the other person. Fragmentation then occurs and the person
does not feel complete unless he or she is with this partner. This is the
attraction a person feels toward a partner after they have sex.

Any type of sexual activity outside the confines of marriage, whether
fornication, adultery, pornography, bestiality, or pedophilia, is
contrary to the Word of God and therefore sin.

"Thou shalt not commit adultery" (Exodus 20:14).

"Do you not know that wrongdoers will not inherit the kingdom of God?
Do not be deceived! Fornicators, idolaters, adulterers, male prostitutes,

sodomites, thieves, the greedy, drunkards, revilers, robbers—none of these will inherit the kingdom of God" (1 Corinthians 6:9–10 NRSV).

Even in rape, incest, or molestation, a strong soul tie is created and must be broken if a person is to be whole in spirit, soul, and body.

During the early Bible era, a couple became one through sexual intimacy just as a couple becomes one today. "Therefore shall a man leave his father and his mother, and shall cleave unto his wife: and they shall be one flesh" (Genesis 2:24).

If you had a sexual encounter prior to your marriage, whether it was in an earlier marriage or in other circumstances, turn to the prayers at the end of this session and repeat the prayer so you can be released from this bondage and become whole not only for your spouse but for God.

Even if you are not married now or have never married, you must still call your spirit and soul back and release those with whom you have been intimately involved.

Do Not Withhold Sex from Your Spouse

> Be ye angry, and sin not: let not the sun go down upon
> your wrath: Neither give place to the devil.
> —Ephesians 4:26–27

Spouses get angry with their mates and withhold affection or sex. When you do this, you are opening the door for Satan to tempt your spouse. And tempt he will, by bringing someone across your mate's path to say just the things he or she wants to hear and to give your spouse the attention you are not providing.

> But because of cases of sexual immorality, each man should
> have his own wife and each woman her own husband. The
> husband should give to his wife her conjugal rights, and

likewise the wife to her husband. For the wife does not
have authority over her own body, but the husband does;
likewise the husband does not have authority over his own
body, but the wife does. Do not deprive one another except
perhaps by agreement for a set time, to devote yourselves
to prayer, and then come together again, so that Satan
may not tempt you because of your lack of self-control. (1
Corinthians 7:2–5 NRSV)

It is impossible to meet all of the emotional and physical needs of more
than one mate no matter how macho a man thinks he is or how wonderful
a woman thinks she is. The person who thinks he or she can live
successfully and find fulfillment outside of a monogamous relationship
in Christ is believing Satan's lies and fooling himself or herself.

A cheating spouse may think he or she is getting away with infidelity,
believing that "what they do not know will not hurt them," But anyone
who accepts this adage does not understand soul ties and the one-
flesh relationship God intended for all marriages. The faithful spouse
knows deep down in the subconscious that something is wrong. The
mate feels alone and unfulfilled in the relationship, but perhaps does
not understand why.

If the unfaithful mate put this misguided energy into his or her spouse
instead of a lover and put God first, the marriage would surely flourish.

Divorce and Sexual Soul Ties

After divorce, we must break soul ties with a former spouse if we want
to be whole in soul and in spirit and ready to live again in one flesh.
Otherwise we may yearn to return to that relationship even if it was
destructive. We must also break any covenant in the spirit realm
regarding past relationships if we want to be completely free.

One of the reasons Christians commit sexual sins is that they do not
know that generational curses and soul ties are operating in their

lives and have not broken them. I will discuss this in more detail in the sections on generational curses.

Destructive Controlling Soul Ties

A destructive soul tie can exist between two people when a controlling demonic spirit exerts itself over another spirit. This Jezebel spirit resides in the person doing the controlling. This spirit is a warring principality, highly deceptive and destructive. I will discuss this spirit in depth in a later study.

Jezebel operates in a person's life from a basis of low self-esteem. The spirit feeds upon this void in the emotions. All the missing emotional traits—a healthy self-esteem, a secure self-identity, a confidence in being loved, and a God-given self-assurance—Jezebel appears to provide, filling all these voids in the emotionally wounded and in those with unresolved childhood issues. Jezebel fools them into believing they are receiving all the things they did not receive in childhood.

This destructive relationship can occur in families or in friendships. An unnatural soul tie develops when one person dominates another to the point that this other person loses control of his or her will. This person cannot control his or her actions and defers to the other person's will. This soul tie must be broken.

"Know ye not, that to whom ye yield yourselves servants to obey, is servants ye are to whom ye obey; whether of sin unto death, or of obedience unto righteousness?" (Romans 6:16).

Unforgiveness

When we hold unforgiveness in our hearts, even if we are unaware it exists, we create an unnatural and unhealthy soul tie with the person or persons we have not forgiven.

"And I will give unto thee the keys of the kingdom of heaven: and whatsoever thou shalt bind on earth shall be bound in heaven: and whatsoever thou shalt loose on earth shall be loosed in heaven" (Matthew 16:19 KJV).

By refusing to release forgiveness, we tie God's hands in the situation and bring the law of reaping and sowing into our lives in this area.

Relationships

We can be tied in dysfunctional ways to many things and have trouble getting free. In many areas of the soul realm, we may be so damaged, fragmented, tied, and bound that we are hindered in moving on with God and achieving wholeness. We have not followed the perfect plan God has for our lives.

God desires restoration and wholeness in our souls and in all other areas of our lives. The mind that is bound to something or someone else cannot be renewed. It is impossible to restore a fragmented mind, a disabled will, or torn and scattered emotions until healing and restoration take place.

A parent and a child can have an unhealthy soul tie. If the parent remains controlling and is enabling a grown child to continue in irresponsibility by not allowing him to reap the consequences of his behavior, there is an unhealthy soul tie between them. The parent may try to justify the help he is giving by saying that if he did not provide it the child or the grandkids would not make it.

If we make help continual rather than temporary, we do not allow our children to grow and to become responsible. Could it be that one of the reasons we have an unhealthy soul tie with a parent or a child is that we are alike in a particular area? This unnatural soul tie is feeding the inadequacies within our own soul realm.

God allows us to reap the consequences of our sinful choices and behaviors. Since the Word of God is our ultimate example, we should also require others to suffer the consequences of their choices. When we reap what we have sown, we quickly learn to change our behaviors lest we go down the same path way again.

If we continue to enable our children or others with whom we have relationships, we prevent them from dealing with their troubles on their own and perhaps changing. Help should be temporary and not constant.

Take the example of a mama's boy. He is involved in an unnatural soul tie; parental inversion may exist. The mother feeds her emotional voids by creating a son who is incapable of existing outside of her control even after he is grown. This type of relationship is labeled codependence.

Such a relationship involves the dependence of two people, groups, or organisms on each other, especially when this reinforces mutually harmful behavior patterns. In this situation, a person such as the partner of an alcoholic or the parent of a drug-addicted child needs to feel needed by the other person.

Three Levels of Soul Ties

1) Intellect
   a) Involvement in the occult can produce dangerous soul ties.
   b) Intellectualism or reliance on psychology can also lead to unhealthy ties.
   c) An inordinate desire for knowledge may also be a problem; Adam and Eve fell because of a wrong desire for knowledge and because they did not trust God.

2) Will
   a) Controlling spirits may be involved; for example, in parent-child, husband-wife, and codependent relationships.

3) Emotions
   a) Soul ties are created in the emotions as well as in the flesh when sex is involved.
   b) Soul ties can be with the same sex or the opposite sex.
   c) An emotional affair can exist with a person of the opposite sex without physical sex, but the relationship can enter the physical realm at a time of weakness.

How to Get Free

1) Ask God to show you any negative soul ties. Pray Psalm 139:23–24.
2) Recognize the problem.
3) Ask for forgiveness for an ungodly/unnatural soul tie.
4) Forgive the other person involved.
5) Ask God to remove the negative/ungodly/unnatural soul tie.
6) Call your fragmented soul and spirit back to yourself.
7) Release the soul and the spirit of the one to whom you were tied.

How to Renew the Mind

Ask God's help in the following way:
1) Recognize the problem. Don't deny it.
2) Reject/rebuke, saying, "In the name of Jesus, I rebuke/reject _____."
3) Replace the unhealthy tie with what the Word says about the situation.
4) Repeat by speaking forth the victory.
5) Reinforce with positive confessions and deliberate actions.

Home Study Guide

Job 32:8; Psalm 42:5-6; 1 Corinthians 15:50; Ecclesiastes 4:9-12; 1 Samuel 18:1; Ruth 1:16; Acts 4:32; Genesis 37:3; Genesis 2:22-23; Ephesians 5:31-32; 1 Corinthians 6:15-20; Exodus 20:14; Genesis 2:24; Romans 6:16; Matthew 16:19; Psalm 139:23-24.

Be perfectly honest with yourself, especially if you are sincere about becoming whole for the Lord. Ask God to show you all hidden negative soul ties. If any thoughts come to mind concerning a relationship, do not ignore them, but pray about them, asking God to reveal His truth regarding the relationship.

- ✗ Have you broken the soul ties from past sexual or marital relationships?
- ✗ Can you think of any relationship or relationships in which you have lost your will and have deferred to others to the detriment of your own wishes?
- ✗ Do you rely on someone else to make the important decisions in your life?
- ✗ Do you share painful emotional experiences with others just to have them side with you and make you feel better?
- ✗ Do you still have emotional pain when you think about hurtful experiences from childhood?

If you answered yes to any of these questions, you may still have a negative soul tie with someone that must be broken. After you have prayed the prayers and processed your emotional scars in part 2, proceed to the prayers for deliverance on the page following this one and let God set you free.

"If the Son therefore shall make you free, ye shall be free indeed" (John 8:36 NKJV).

The first *free* in this passage means to liberate, to exempt, to deliver, to make free. The second *free* means unrestrained, acting not as a slave but as a citizen, exempt from obligation or liability, at liberty.

So you can see the implied image is total freedom in every way; the first *free* points to the price Christ paid to liberate us from the penalty of eternal death due to humanity's sinful nature.

The next *free* indicates that we should have no restraint in enjoying our freedom in Christ as we are no longer slaves to sin.

Jesus wants to set us completely free from dysfunctional behavioral patterns so we can become all He has called us to be in Him!

Prayer for Deliverance

Father, I come to You in the name of Jesus. I ask Your forgiveness for all sexual encounters I have had in my past that were outside of the bounds of marriage. I ask You to release me from all past unnatural soul ties. I call back the fragments of my soul and my spirit unto myself from past encounters, whether they were in or outside of marriage, making me complete and whole, presenting myself to You without reservation. I release soul and spirit ties with these people, commanding them to return to their owners.

I release forgiveness to _____. (Place the name of the person/persons who hurt you in any of the above relationships.) I ask You to forgive me for holding _____ (name the incident) against them and for judging them in the situation.

(If these people are still alive, pray this as well.)

I ask You to not hold this sin against them, because they did not know what they were doing. Father, I ask You to bless them, sending laborers across their paths to open their eyes to Your truth. Amen.

Notes

Notes

Generational Curses I

Part 5

Origination of Curses

God cursed the earth and all humanity because Adam and Eve disobeyed His command not to eat of the Tree of Knowledge of Good and Evil.

> And the Lord God said unto the serpent, Because thou hast done this, thou art cursed above all cattle, and above every beast of the field; upon thy belly shalt thou go, and dust shalt thou eat all the days of thy life: And I will put enmity between thee and the woman, and between thy seed and her seed; it shall bruise thy head, and thou shalt bruise his heel. Unto the woman he said, I will greatly multiply thy sorrow and thy conception; in sorrow thou shalt bring forth children; and thy desire shall be to thy husband, and he shall rule over thee.

> And unto Adam he said, Because thou hast hearkened unto the voice of thy wife, and hast eaten of the tree; of which I commanded thee, saying, Thou shalt not eat of it: cursed is the ground for thy sake; in sorrow shalt thou eat of it all the days of thy life; thorns also and thistles shall it bring forth to thee; and thou shalt eat the herb of the field; in the sweat of thy face shalt thou eat bread, till thou return unto the

ground; for out of it wast thou taken: for dust thou art, and unto dust shalt thou return. (Genesis 3:14–19 KJV)

All the evil found in the world today originated in the garden of Eden. This era will end when Christ returns, riding His white horse, the saints of glory with Him, to fight the battle of Armageddon.

Many Christians believe curses do not apply to them since Christ became a curse for us. Part of this assumption is indeed correct, but part is not. Keep an open mind and see this study through to the end, allowing the Word of God to speak for itself. God calls us to study His Word and to correctly understand His truth.

"Study to show thyself approved unto God, a workman that needeth not to be ashamed, rightly dividing the word of truth" (2 Timothy 2:15 KJV).

When we study the Word of God, we must first discern who is speaking, to whom the person speaking, and the context of the words. We must always remember that the Word of God discerns or interprets the Word of God. Therefore removing or isolating a Scripture passage to prove a point is heresy.

Let's delve into the Word of God and see what it says concerning curses.

God's Covenant of Blessings with Abraham

God told Abraham that all his descendants and all nations would be blessed through him in an everlasting covenant.

"And I will make thee exceeding fruitful, and I will make nations of thee, and kings shall come out of thee. And I will establish my covenant between me and thee and thy seed after thee in their generations for an everlasting covenant, to be a God unto thee, and to thy seed after thee. And I will give unto thee, and to thy seed after thee, the land wherein thou art a stranger, all the land of Canaan, for an everlasting possession; and I will be their God" (Genesis 17:6–8 KJV).

God's Covenant with Abraham Applies to Us Today

Abraham obtained the promises of God through faith and not through the law.

> For the promise, that he should be the heir of the world, was not to Abraham, or to his seed, through the law, but through the righteousness of faith. For if they which are of the law be heirs, faith is made void, and the promise made of none effect: Because the law worketh wrath: for where no law is, there is no transgression. Therefore it is of faith, that it might be by grace; to the end the promise might be sure to all the seed; not to that only which is of the law, but to that also which is of the faith of Abraham; who is the father of us all. (Romans 4:13-16 KJV).

"And if ye be Christ's, then are ye Abraham's seed, and heirs according to the promise" (Galatians 3:29 KJV).

Christians say that the Old Testament is not for us today and that it applied only to the people of the Old Testament. Galatians 3:29 in the New Testament says that the blessings of Abraham are ours today.

"Abraham had the same experience—God declared him fit for heaven only because he believed God's promises. You can see from this that the real children of Abraham are all the men of faith who truly trust in God. What's more, the Scriptures looked forward to this time when God would save the Gentiles also, through their faith. God told Abraham about this long ago when he said, 'I will bless those in every nation who trust in me as you do.' And so it is: all who trust in Christ share the same blessing Abraham received" (Galatians 3:6–9 Life Application: The Living Translation).

Abraham's Blessings Continue

> And it shall come to pass, if thou shalt hearken
> diligently unto the voice of the Lord thy God, to observe
> and to do all his commandments which I command thee
> this day, that the Lord thy God will set thee on high above
> all nations of the earth: And all these blessings shall come
> on thee, and overtake thee, if thou shalt hearken unto the
> voice of the Lord thy God. Blessed shalt thou be in the city,
> and blessed shalt thou be in the field.
>
> —Deuteronomy 28:1–14 KJV

The blessings bestowed upon Abraham apply to us if only we obey God's Word.

Curses

A curse is "a prayer of invocation for harm or injury to come upon one; evil or misfortune that comes as if in response to imprecation or as retribution; a cause of great harm of misfortune." To curse is to "use profanely insolent language against, blaspheme; to call upon divine or supernatural power to send injury upon; to execrate in fervent and often profane terms; to bring great evil upon, afflict." (*Webster's Collegiate Dictionary, Electronic Edition, 1994, 1995*)

Curses from disobedience apply to all generations following Abraham. "And they shall be upon thee for a sign and for a wonder, and upon thy seed forever" (Deuteronomy 28:46 KJV).

Most people believe Christ delivered them from curses when He died on the cross of Calvary. That is indeed so. But let's look at this subject a little more deeply and rightly divide the Word of God.

Christ Delivered Us from the Curse

> Christ hath redeemed us from the curse of the law, being made a curse for us: for it is written, Cursed is every one that hangeth on a tree: That the blessing of Abraham might come on the Gentiles through Jesus Christ; that we might receive the promise of the Spirit through faith.
>
> —Galatians 3:13–14 KJV

> Who his own self bare our sins in his own body on the tree, that we, being dead to sins, should live unto righteousness: by whose stripes ye were healed.
>
> —1 Peter 2:24 KJV

We are not automatically delivered from curses by Christ's death and resurrection until we appropriate His promises.

If being born again offers automatic deliverance from the curses, why do Christians still have to suffer death? Were these problems all a result of the sin of Adam and Eve? Didn't the fall result in spiritual and physical death and in disease and force men to work by the sweat of their brows and women to bear children in pain? Didn't we lose face-to-face communication with God because of this fall?

If new birth in Christ results in automatic deliverance, why are we not instantly perfect the way Adam and Eve were in the garden before the fall?

Even after we are born again, God gives us a choice about how we will live. Will we live as over comers or will we live defeated lives?

"I am the gate; whoever enters through me will be saved. He will come in and go out, and find pasture. The thief comes only to steal and kill and destroy; I have come that they may have life, and have it to the full. I am the good shepherd. The good shepherd lays down his life for the sheep" (John 10:9–11 NIV).

If we were automatically free from the effects of the curse brought by Adam and Eve's disobedience, the Bible verses above would not be necessary. Why would God warn His people to beware of Satan's ability to steal, kill, and destroy what Christ has so freely paid for us to have?

A Baby Born into This World Is Not Born Again

A baby is not given a born-again spirit at birth and is not automatically saved. Children must reach the age of accountability and receive Jesus into their hearts for themselves. They must acknowledge their sins, apply the blood of Jesus to their lives, and confess the price He paid.

Do not misunderstand. Children who die before reaching the age of accountability will go to heaven.

All humanity still labors under the curse of sin. When Christ said, "It is finished," and died on the cross, He defeated hell and Satan and took back what was stolen from Adam and Even in the garden of Eden. He gave these victories to His church, the body of Christ.

We Must Take by Force What Belongs to Us

Satan is not going to roll over and play dead while we go about life with everything Jesus gained for us on the cross. Everything Jesus won for us was taken by force from Satan in the spirit realm before it was manifested in the natural realm.

"And from the days of John the Baptist until now the kingdom of heaven suffereth violence, and the violent take it by force" (Matthew 11:12).

God Gives Us a Choice

I call heaven and earth as witnesses today against you, that I have set before you life and death, blessing

and cursing; therefore choose life, that both you and your
descendants may live.
—Deuteronomy 30:19 KJV

If we choose our own way, God removes His hand of protection from
us, allowing Satan to accomplish evil in our lives. His only motive is
to bring us to the revelation that we can do nothing without Him and
to restore our relationship with Him—the fellowship Adam and Eve
enjoyed before the fall. God does not put illness or tragedy upon us.
There is no sin or illness in heaven. Satan alone comes to steal, to kill,
and to destroy.

"The thief cometh not, but for to steal, and to kill, and to destroy: I
am come that they might have life, and that they might have it more
abundantly" (John 10:10 KJV).

Curses Have Causes

As the bird by wandering, as the swallow by flying, so
the curse causeless shall not come.
—Proverbs 26:2 KJV

For a curse to take effect upon someone, there must be a foundation
of sin in that person's life in the particular area of the curse.

Sin in our hearts is an open door for Satan to inflict curses upon us.
The sins of our ancestors can also bring curses upon us even if we are
innocent. Do you remember the consequences for disobedience that
God detailed in Deuteronomy 28? He said all these curses would result
from disobedience. When a person sins, he opens the door for a demon
spirit to oppress not only himself but the following generations. This
spirit will cause the next generation to sin in similar ways. Thus the
iniquity will be passed down to the fourth and the fifth generations.

If a seed falls on cement, it will not germinate and grow. Without soil
and adequate water, it cannot take root and will die. No one cannot

speak a curse over us unless we have the fertile soil of sin in our lives! If we are in the blood of Jesus and have no sin, a curse cannot take root.

"And he took up his parable, and said, Balak the king of Moab hath brought me from Aram, out of the mountains of the east, saying, Come, curse me Jacob, and come, defy Israel. How shall I curse, whom God hath not cursed? or how shall I defy, whom the Lord hath not defied?" (Numbers 23:7–8 KJV).

Balak, king of the Moabites, was afraid of the children of Israel because they were so numerous. He was also afraid because God had been with them in conquering the Amorites. Therefore he sent for Balaam to curse the people of Israel. But because the favor of God was with them, Balaam could not curse them.

Curses upon Our Seed

Cursed shall be the fruit of thy body.
—Deuteronomy 28:18 KJV

Moreover all these curses shall come upon thee, and shall pursue thee, and overtake thee, till thou be destroyed; because thou hearkenedst not unto the voice of the lord thy God, to keep his commandments and his statutes which he commanded thee: And they shall be upon thee for a sign and for a wonder, and upon thy seed for ever. Because thou servedst not the Lord thy God with joyfulness, and with gladness of heart, for the abundance of all things.
—Deuteronomy 28:45–47 KJV

Keeping mercy for thousands, forgiving iniquity and transgression and sin, and that will by no means clear the guilty; visiting the iniquity of the fathers upon the children, and upon the children's children, unto the third and to the fourth generation.
—Exodus 34:7 KJV

> Keeping steadfast love for the thousandth generation,
> forgiving iniquity and transgression and sin, yet by no
> means clearing the guilty, but visiting the iniquity of the
> parents upon the children and the children's children, to
> the third and the fourth generation.
>
> —Exodus 34:7 NRSV

Iniquity is the sinful nature that Adam and Eve received as a result of disobeying God's command not to eat of the Tree of Knowledge of Good and Evil. Their disobedience yielded spiritual death and the carnal nature that all humanity possesses. This nature created a propensity to sin. They lost the glory of God that clothed them and realized that they were naked. They were without God's covering and no longer experienced His manifested presence.

Hidden unconfessed sins produce repeated manifestations of sin in our lives whether these sins are known or unknown. This habitual offense becomes an iniquity, which results in a generational curse by God. The curse is the result of unconfessed sin/sins, which creates an open door for demonic spirits to bring fulfillment of the curse.

These curses are due to disobedience. The person sins, opening the door for a demon spirit to oppress not only the person who sinned but the following generations as well. This spirit will cause the next generation to sin in similar ways; thus the iniquity is passed down to the third and fourth generations, as these Bible passages note.

We may continue to labor under generational curses because of a lack of knowledge.

Manifestations of Curses

Manifestations include physical and mental illness, suicide, alcoholism, drug addiction, divorce, a perverse spirit (which includes all sexual sin such as incest, homosexuality, pornography, adultery, fornication, and bestiality), poverty, physical abuse, relationship dysfunction, rage, food addictions, overspending, and addiction to approval. Inherited curses can also affect churches, nations, states, cities, geographical regions, or entire families. The list is endless.

Ways We Perpetuate Generational Curses

1. By being ignorant of curses operating in our families.
2. By judging our authority figure/figures for the pain inflicted upon us by the manifestation of the curse or the curses in our families.
3. By holding unforgiveness toward the authority figure/figures for the manifestation of the curse that caused disruption or pain in our lives.
4. By believing that the dysfunctional lifestyle produced by the curse/curses is normal for our families.
5. By transferring the evil spirit and causing the curse to continue.

Notes

Generational Curses II

Part 6

> All scripture is given by inspiration of God, and is profitable for doctrine, for reproof, for correction, for instruction in righteousness.
>
> —2 Timothy 3:16

This verse found in the New Testament shows that the whole Bible remains relevant to this day.

"But when the fullness of the time was come, God sent forth his Son, made of a woman, made under the law, to redeem them that were under the law, that we might receive the adoption of sons" (Galatians 4:4–5 KJV).

"Think not that I am come to destroy the law, or the prophets: I am not come to destroy, but to fulfill. For verily I say unto you, till heaven and earth pass, one jot or one tittle shall in no wise pass from the law, till all be fulfilled" (Matthew 5:17–18 KJV).

We no longer live under the law given to the nation of Israel. Jesus fulfilled the law and set us free under the new covenant of grace bought by His blood. However, the spiritual principles found in the Old Testament are still true for us today.

Read Matthew 5:17–48. Here Jesus is saying we must go beyond the law, not do away with it. Our love for Christ must be the force that allows us to proceed past the written law to fulfill a heart-felt desire for Him in our lives. What must act according to the heart, not because someone has told us what to do. In verse 44, Jesus tells us we must "love our enemies, bless them that curse you, do good to them that hate you, and pray for them which despitefully use you and persecute you." In doing this, we go past the law, allowing Christ to transform us.

"Who also hath made us able ministers of the new testament not of the letter, but of the spirit: for the letter killeth, but the spirit giveth life" (2 Corinthians 3:6 KJV).

Ignorance of Curses

Curses affect us whether or not we know about them!

"My people are destroyed for lack of knowledge" (Hosea 4:6 KJV).

"Therefore my people have gone into captivity, because they have no knowledge; their honorable men are famished, and their multitude dried up with thirst" (Isaiah 5:13 KJV).

"For wisdom is a defense as money is a defense, but the excellence of knowledge is that wisdom gives life to those who have it" (Ecclesiastes 7:12 KJV).

"Lest Satan should take advantage of us; for we are not ignorant of his devices" (2 Corinthians 2:11 KJV).

We cannot fight a battle we do not know exists. We cannot defeat an enemy when we do not even know he is attacking us. But ignorance is no excuse. God holds us accountable for everything that is in His Word.

Sources of Curses

The two major defining characteristics of humans are their free will and their power of speech. God created the universe with His spoken word. In like manner, we create with our words whether they are positive or negative.

"Death and life are in the power of the tongue: and they that love it shall eat the fruit thereof" (Proverbs 18:21 KJV).

The Breaking of God's Laws Is Sin

> Will a man rob God? Yet ye have robbed me. But ye say, wherein have we robbed thee? In tithes and offerings. Ye are cursed with a curse: for ye have robbed me, even this whole nation. Bring ye all the tithes into the storehouse, that there may be meat in mine house, and prove me now herewith, saith the Lord of hosts, if I will not open you the windows of heaven, and pour you out a blessing, that there shall not be room enough to receive it.
> —Malachi 3:8–10 KJV

If we don't give God the 10 percent He requires, we will be cursed by Him.

"Now the Lord had said unto Abram, Get thee out of thy country, and from thy kindred, and from thy father's house, unto a land that I will shew thee: And I will make of thee a great nation, and I will bless thee, and make thy name great; and thou shalt be a blessing: And I will bless them that bless thee, and curse him that curseth thee: and in thee shall all families of the earth be blessed" (Genesis 2:1–3 KJV).

Watch the words of your mouth against God's children.

Consider Achan's sin of disobedience. Joshua 6 describes how the children of Israel took the city of Jericho. God had told them to collect the silver, the gold, and the vessels of brass and of iron for the treasury of the house of the Lord. Chapter 7 recounts how Achan disobeyed and took a Babylonian garment (representing worldly gain), two hundred shekels of silver (one shekel equals sixty-five cents), and a wedge of gold fifty shekels in weight.

This sin of one Israelite defiled the people as a whole and they lost the battle of Ai following their victory at Jericho. Achan had thwarted the will of God not only for himself, but for his people by his sin of disobedience.

Every tribe of Israel appeared before Joshua where Achan confessed his sin in taking the forbidden items. All Israel stoned Achan as well as his sons, his daughters, and those of his household. Then the people burned everything that pertained to him including animals, household goods, his tent, and all the stolen items.

Do not believe for one moment that our sins do not affect others, because the book of Joshua shows us otherwise.

The book of Genesis tells us how Rachel stole her father Laban's gods, or idols, and how Jacob cursed the person who stole them.

"Now Laban had gone to shear his sheep, and Rachel stole her father's household gods. And Jacob deceived Laban the Aramean, in that he did not tell him that he intended to flee" (Genesis 31:19–20 NRSV).

"'Even though you had to go because you longed greatly for your father's house, why did you steal my gods?' Jacob answered Laban, 'Because I was afraid, for I thought that you would take your daughters from me by force. But anyone with whom you find your gods shall not live. In the presence of our kinsfolk, point out what I have that is yours, and take it.' Now Jacob did not know that Rachel had stolen the gods" (Genesis 31:30–32 NRSV). [Emphasis mine]

The idols that Rachel stole from her father were used in the worship of heathen gods. God forbids us to have anything in our possession pertaining to the worship of other gods! Because of the curse that

Jacob spoke, Rachel died while giving birth to Joseph. Do not think for a minute our words are not important.

"And they journeyed from Bethel; and there was but a little way to come to Ephrath: and Rachel travailed, and she had hard labour.

And it came to pass, when she was in hard labour, that the midwife said unto her, Fear not; thou shalt have this son also.

And it came to pass, as her soul was in departing, (for she died) that she called his name Benoni: but his father called him Benjamin.

And Rachel died, and was buried in the way to Ephrath, which is Bethlehem." (Genesis 35:16–19 KJV).

Put sin far from you and God will fight for you!

> God said to Jacob, "Arise, go up to Bethel, and settle there. Make an altar there to the God who appeared to you when you fled from your brother Esau." So Jacob said to his household and to all who were with him, "Put away the foreign gods that are among you, and purify yourselves, and change your clothes; then come, let us go up to Bethel, that I may make an altar there to the God who answered me in the day of my distress and has been with me wherever I have gone."
>
> So they gave to Jacob all the foreign gods that they had, and the rings that were in their ears; and Jacob hid them under the oak that was near Shechem. As they journeyed, a terror from God fell upon the cities all around them, so that no one pursued them. (Genesis 35:1–5 KJV) [Emphasis mine]

"The images of their gods you are to burn in the fire. Do not covet the silver and gold on them, and do not take it for yourselves, or you will be ensnared by it, for it is detestable to the Lord your God. Do not bring a detestable thing into your house or you, like it, will be set apart for destruction. Utterly abhor and detest it, for it is set apart for destruction" (Deuteronomy 7:25–26 NIV).

Do not even try to melt down the gold or the silver and mold it into some other piece of jewelry. God's Word tells us to destroy it!

Open Doors for Curses

We give Satan an invitation to attack us when we become involved in situations that give him entrance into our lives. We can do this knowingly or unknowingly. To remove the curse or curses, we must repent and be cleansed. Here are some means by which curses fall upon us.

- Through persons with relational authority—relatives, employers, doctors, teachers
  a) A doctor may give us a bad report or prognosis.
  b) Parents or teachers tell us that we are stupid and will never amount to anything.
  c) We offer repeated spoken agreement with the prognosis and assent to the harsh judgment of a parent or a teacher instead of speaking the truth of God's Word concerning our circumstances.

- Through ourselves
  a) We speak negative words.
  b) We are guilty of hatred, unforgiveness, jealousy, and the misspoken word.
  c) We have wrong eating habits.

- Through inheritance
  a) Predisposition through our genes.
  b) Sins of our forefathers.
  c) Ancestors' acceptance of curses on the lives of descendants.

d) Continuing in the sins of our forefathers.

- Through involvement with unclean and unholy things
  a) Bringing cursed objects into the home or the office.
  b) Handling unholy things.
  c) Giving honor to demon gods.
  d) Following demonic fads.

- Through territorial rights violations
  a) Touching Satan's ground.
  b) Answering Satan's attacks with railings rather than the Word.
  c) Living on unclean or cursed land or in unclean or cursed housing.

- Through performance of demonic rituals
  a) Executing occultic drawings.
  b) Directly engaging the spirit realm.
  c) Using demonic items.

Purposes of Curses

1. Curses sent by Satan or his servants are always intended to cause injury, loss, destruction, or death.
2. Curses sent by God are intended to gain a person's attention and cause him to turn from his evil ways and toward God and to purify his life.

Curses sent by Satan always involve demon spirits sent to a person or a family for a specific purpose.

> *Sin is always the vehicle demons use to bring the fulfillment of a curse into our lives.*

The Bible offers examples of curses.

In Deuteronomy 28:1-15, God told the children of Israel about the blessings that would come if they obeyed His voice. In Deuteronomy 28:15-68, He detailed the curses that would befall them if they did not obey.

Here are some of the curses from disobedience.

"But it shall come to pass, if thou wilt not hearken unto the voice of the Lord thy God, to observe to do all his commandments and his statutes which I command thee this day; that all these curses shall come upon thee, and overtake thee: Cursed shalt thou be in the city, and cursed shalt thou be in the field. Cursed shall be thy basket and thy store" (Deuteronomy 28:15–17 KJV).

What they eat would be cursed.

"Cursed shall be the fruit of thy body, and the fruit of thy land, the increase of thy kine, and the flocks of thy sheep" (Deuteronomy 28:18 KJV).

The Israelites would suffer barren wombs and cursed children. Their work would not be profitable; livestock was equivalent to wealth in Bible days.

"The Lord shall smite thee with a consumption, and with a fever, and with an inflammation, with an extreme burning, and with the sword, and with blasting, and with mildew; and they shall pursue thee until thou perish" Deuteronomy 28:22 KJV).

The people would be afflicted with bad health (sin produces sickness) and would lose favor with everyone around them.

I have discussed only a few curses listed in the Bible, but I believe every area of our lives is represented in the curses mentioned in Deuteronomy 28:16-68.

The only true source of knowledge is the Father, the Son, and the Holy Spirit. Ask God to show you any generational curses that exist in your family. God expects you to do something about the situation. He won't do it for you. It's not necessary to know the specific sin or sins of your ancestors. Come to the Father in the name of Jesus and simply ask Him to forgive the sin or the sins that caused the curse or the curses.

"Behold, I give unto you power to tread on serpents and scorpions, and over all the power of the enemy: and nothing shall by any means hurt you" (Luke 10:19 KJV).

Consider Abraham and King Abimelech in Genesis 20:1–12.

> From there Abraham journeyed toward the region of the Negeb, and settled between Kadesh and Shur. While residing in Gerar as an alien, Abraham said of his wife Sarah, "She is my sister." And King Abimelech of Gerar sent and took Sarah.

> But God came to Abimelech in a dream by night, and said to him, "You are about to die because of the woman whom you have taken; for she is a married woman."

> Now Abimelech had not approached her; so he said, "Lord, will you destroy an innocent people? Did he not himself say to me, 'She is my sister'? And she herself said, 'He is my brother.' I did this in the integrity of my heart and the innocence of my hands."

> Then God said to him in the dream, "Yes, I know that you did this in the integrity of your heart; furthermore it was I who kept you from sinning against me. Therefore I did not let you touch her. Now then, return the man's wife; for he is a prophet, and he will pray for you and you shall live. But if you do not restore her, know that you shall surely die, you and all that are yours."

So Abimelech rose early in the morning, and called all his servants and told them all these things; and the men were very much afraid. Then Abimelech called Abraham, and said to him, "What have you done to us? How have I sinned against you, that you have brought such great guilt on me and my kingdom? You have done things to me that ought not to be done."

And Abimelech said to Abraham, "What were you thinking of, that you did this thing?"
Abraham said, "I did it because I thought, There is no fear of God at all in this place, and they will kill me because of my wife. Besides, she is indeed my sister, the daughter of my father but not the daughter of my mother; and she became my wife."

Pray for others and God will heal you.

So Abraham prayed unto God: and God healed Abimelech, and his wife, and his maidservants; and they bore children (Genesis 20:17 KJV). [Emphasis mine]

Abraham and Sarah went to the land of Gerar where he told King Abimelech that Sarah was his sister, a half-truth. The king took Sarah into his palace to be one of his wives. In a dream God told Abimelech that if he did not return Sarah to Abraham his kingdom would be destroyed. So the king took Sarah back to Abraham and asked Abraham to pray for him and his nation because God had cursed him and his people.

Generational Curse, Abraham to Isaac

Isaac lied about his wife Rebekah just as Abraham lied about Sarah his wife being his sister.

Now there was a famine in the land, besides the former famine that had occurred in the days of Abraham. And Isaac went to Gerar, to King Abimelech of the Philistines. The Lord appeared to Isaac and said, "Do not go down to Egypt; settle in the land that I shall show you. Reside in this land as an alien, and I will be with you, and will bless you; for to you and to your descendants I will give all these lands, and I will fulfill the oath that I swore to your father Abraham.

I will make your offspring as numerous as the stars of heaven, and will give to your offspring all these lands; and all the nations of the earth shall gain blessing for themselves through your offspring, because Abraham obeyed my voice and kept my charge, my commandments, my statutes, and my laws."

So Isaac settled in Gerar. When the men of the place asked him about his wife, he said, "She is my sister"; for he was afraid to say, "My wife," thinking, "or else the men of the place might kill me for the sake of Rebekah, because she is attractive in appearance."

When Isaac had been there a long time, King Abimelech of the Philistines looked out of a window and saw him fondling his wife Rebekah. So Abimelech called for Isaac, and said, "So she is your wife! Why then did you say, 'She is my sister'?" Isaac said to him, "Because I thought I might die because of her."

Abimelech said, "What is this you have done to us? One of the people might easily have lain with your wife, and you would have brought guilt upon us."

So Abimelech warned all the people, saying, "Whoever touches this man or his wife shall be put to death. (Genesis 26:1–11)

Now consider Saul's sin.

> And Samuel said, When thou wast little in thine own sight,
> wast thou not made the head of the tribes of Israel, and
> the Lord anointed thee king over Israel?" And the Lord sent
> thee on a journey, and said, Go and utterly destroy the
> sinners the Amalekites, and fight against them until they
> be consumed. Wherefore then didst thou not obey the voice
> of the Lord, but didst fly upon the spoil, and didst evil in the
> sight of the Lord?
>
> And Saul said unto Samuel, Yea, I have obeyed the voice of
> the Lord, and have gone the way which the Lord sent me,
> and have brought Agag the king of Amalek, and have utterly
> destroyed the Amalekites.
> But the people took of the spoil, sheep and oxen, the chief
> of the things which should have been utterly destroyed, to
> sacrifice unto the Lord thy God in Gilgal.
>
> And Samuel said, Hath the Lord as great delight in burnt
> offerings and sacrifices, as in obeying the voice of the Lord?
> Behold, to obey is better than sacrifice, and to hearken than
> the fat of rams.
> For rebellion is as the sin of witchcraft, and stubbornness
> is as iniquity and idolatry. Because thou hast rejected the
> word of the Lord, he hath also rejected thee from being king.
> And Saul said unto Samuel, I have sinned: for I have
> transgressed the commandment of the Lord, and thy words:
> <u>because I feared the people, and obeyed their voice</u>." (1
> Samuel 15:17–24 KJV) [Emphasis mine]

Saul was more concerned with his self-image and with what people
thought about him than with what God thought about him; he was
more concerned about the accolades of men, more concerned about
being popular than about pleasing God. Saul was a people pleaser and
received his affirmations from men instead of from God.

Saul did not know who he was in God or how to achieve a relationship with the Father. Saul's spirit had perhaps been wounded in early childhood, resulting in low self-esteem. Because of this low self-esteem, he received the image of who he was from the people surrounding him.

> This I say then, Walk in the Spirit, and ye shall not fulfil the lust of the flesh. For the flesh lusteth against the Spirit, and the Spirit against the flesh: and these are contrary the one to the other: so that ye cannot do the things that ye would. But if ye be led of the Spirit, ye are not under the law.

> Now the works of the flesh are manifest, which are these; Adultery, fornication, uncleanness, lasciviousness, Idolatry, witchcraft, hatred, variance, emulations, wrath, strife, seditions, heresies, Envyings, murders, drunkenness, revellings, and such like: of the which I tell you before, as I have also told you in time past, that they which do such things shall not inherit the kingdom of God. (Galations 5:22-25 KJV)

> But the fruit of the Spirit is love, joy, peace, longsuffering, gentleness, goodness, faith, meekness, temperance: against such there is no law. And they that are Christ's have crucified the flesh with the affections and lusts. If we live in the Spirit, let us also walk in the Spirit. (Galatians 5:22-25 KJV).

It is not possible to please God and human beings at the same time. We must choose whom we will serve. If we choose God, He can and will meet all our needs, restoring our fellowship with the Trinity as well as bringing restoration to our spirit, soul, and body.

> Now therefore fear the Lord, and serve him in sincerity and in truth: and put away the gods which your fathers served on the other side of the flood, and in Egypt; and serve ye the Lord. And if it seem evil unto you to serve the

LORD, choose you this day whom ye will serve; whether the gods which your fathers served that were on the other side of the flood, or the gods of the Amorites, in whose land ye dwell: but as for me and my house, we will serve the LORD (Joshua 24:14-15 KJV).

Involvement with Unclean and Unholy Things

Handling unclean objects, bringing certain items into our homes, and engaging in occult practices can allow demons to gain entrance where they otherwise might not have. Listed below are several of those objects and practices and why they are harmful.

Dream catchers: Native Americans believe that the night air is filled with dreams both good and bad. Hung over or near your bed and swinging freely in the air, the dream catcher captures the dreams as they flow by. The good dreams know how to pass through the dream catcher, slipping through the outer holes and sliding down the soft feathers so gently that many times the sleeper does not know that he or she is dreaming. The bad dreams, not knowing the way, get tangled in the dream catcher and perish with the first light of the new day. Using a dream catcher is sinful because it depends upon something or someone other than the God of Abraham, Isaac, and Jacob, creator of all things.

Peace symbol: This is an ancient and powerful symbol of the Antichrist. During the dark ages it was used in Druid witchcraft and by satanists of all sorts during the initiation of new members to their orders. They would draw the magic circle and give the initiate a cross. The initiate would lift the cross and turn it upside down. He would then renounce Christianity in the past, the present, and the future and break the horizontal pieces downward, forming the design of the raven's foot. This ugly symbol is nothing short of blasphemy against the Holy Ghost. To wear or to display this symbol is to announce knowingly or unknowingly that you have rejected Christ. Symbolism is a picture language, and a picture is worth a thousand words.

> Think not that I am come to destroy the law, or the prophets: I am not come to destroy, but to fulfill. For verily I say unto you, Till heaven and earth pass, one jot or one tittle shall in no wise pass from the law, till all be fulfilled.
>
> Whosoever therefore shall break one of these least commandments, and shall teach men so, he shall be called the least in the kingdom of heaven: but whosoever shall do and teach them, the same shall be called great in the kingdom of heaven. For I say unto you, That except your righteousness shall exceed the righteousness of the scribes and Pharisees, ye shall in no case enter into the kingdom of heaven (Matthew 5:17-20 KJV).

Christ did not come to do away with the law but to fulfill it. We are living under the dispensation of grace. Therefore what we do or don't do must go beyond the law of the prophets to love for and obedience to God.

> But if ye be led of the Spirit, ye are not under the law (Galatians 5:18 KJV).

This verse indicates that if we adhere to the sins of the flesh we are still under the law of the prophets. If we live by the flesh, we will never obey God or fulfill His purpose in our lives because we can never obey the law without sinning.

Pentagrams: These are symbols used in satanic worship. There are numerous symbols used in pagan and satanic worship. Ask God to show you these symbols as they are too numerous to list here. You can search the Internet with the words "demonic symbols," and a vast array of symbols used in the occult will appear for you to see. However, do not print out these symbols and leave them lying around your home, since this would be a point of contact for demons to enter your home and oppress not only you but everyone living there, including your pets.

Witchcraft: Dungeons and Dragons, ouija boards, or any other games, videos, or books depicting witchcraft, whether it is white witchcraft or black magic, are not conducive to a Christ-like way of life and are therefore strictly forbidden by the Word of God.

Séances, fortune-tellers, horoscopes, psychics, clairvoyants, spiritualists, soothsayers, diviners, mediums, stargazing, tarot reading, and feng-shui are fueled by familiar spirits called demons and are straight from the pits of hell and Satan himself.

These familiar spirits are entering our children's world through cartoons, games, and seemingly innocent toys. Please take time from your busy life to educate yourself and police your child's activities as well as your own. Be an example in word and in deed for your household concerning this issue.

> Manasseh was twelve years old when he began to reign, and he reigned fifty and five years in Jerusalem:² But did that which was evil in the sight of the LORD, like unto the abominations of the heathen, whom the LORD had cast out before the children of Israel. For he built again the high places which Hezekiah his father had broken down, and he reared up altars for Baalim, and made groves, and worshipped all the host of heaven, and served them. Also he built altars in the house of the LORD, whereof the LORD had said, In Jerusalem shall my name be forever.
>
> And he built altars for all the host of heaven in the two courts of the house of the LORD. And he caused his children to pass through the fire in the valley of the son of Hinnom: also he observed times, and used enchantments, and used witchcraft, and dealt with a familiar spirit, and with wizards: he wrought much evil in the sight of the LORD, to provoke him to anger (2 Chronicles 33:1-6 KJV).

Halloween: "Hallowe'en or All Hallows Eve, the name given to Oct. 31, as the vigil of Hallowmas or All Saints' Day, now chiefly known as the eve of the Christian festival. It long antedates Christianity. The two chief characteristics of ancient Hallowe'en were the lighting of bonfires and the belief that this is the one night in the year during which ghosts and witches are most likely to wander abroad. History shows that the main celebrations of Hallowe'en were purely Druidical (a man who worships and celebrates the forces of nature), and this is further proved by the fact that in parts of Ireland Oct. 31 is still known as Oidhche Shamhna, 'Vigil of Sama.' This is directly connected with the Druidic belief in the calling together of certain wicked souls on Hallowe'en by Saman, lord of death." (*Encyclopedia Britannica 14th Edition*)

"And have no fellowship with the unfruitful works of darkness, but rather reprove them" (Ephesians 5:11 KJV).

"Abstain from all appearance of evil" (1 Thessalonians 5:22 KJV).

> When thou art come into the land which the Lord thy God giveth thee, thou shalt not learn to do after the abominations of those nations. There shall not be found among you any one that maketh his son or his daughter to pass through the fire, or that useth divination, or an observer of time, or an enchanter, or a witch, or a charmer, or a consulter with familiar spirits, or a wizard, or a necromancer [one who attempts to communicate with the spirits of the dead in order to predict or influence the future]. For all that do these things are an abomination unto the Lord: and because of these abominations the Lord thy God doth drive them out from before thee. (Deuteronomy 18:9–12 KJV)

Deuteronomy 18 strictly forbade the people of Israel from having anything to do with the satanic practices of their Canaanite neighbors. This scriptural principle still applies to us today.

"Regard not them that have familiar spirits, neither seek after wizards, to be defiled by them; I am the Lord your God" (Leviticus 19:31 KJV).

"And many that believed came, and confessed, and shewed their deeds. Many of them also which used curious arts brought their books together, and burned them before all men: and they counted the price of them, and found it fifty thousand pieces of silver" (Acts 19:18–19 KJV).

Mardi Gras: Mardi Gras celebrations originated in pagan pre-Christian celebrations of spring. Ancient Greeks would sacrifice a goat, cut its hide in strips, and run naked through the fields while a pagan priest lashed them with goat-hide strips. This ritual was part of the spring fertility rite intended to ensure a productive harvest and to increase the fertility of women and flocks. It was a time of lewdness, immorality, drunkenness, and revelry associated with the worship of the Greek god Pan.

Pan was a Greek fertility god of the fields, the cattle, the herds, and the flocks. He was represented as crude, wanton, and lustful. His form was half goat and half man, having the legs, ears, and horns of a goat (the ancient symbol of Satan), but the torso, arms, and face of a man.

The early church considered this tradition evil, but as time progressed, the purity and the godliness of the church become compromised. Since church leaders could not suppress this evil tradition, they instead absorbed it. The church made the spring rites an acceptable feast before the Lenten season of penance and abstinence and called it *carnelevare*, a Latin word meaning "farewell to the flesh." This festival proceeded the period of fasting.

Mythological gods: In Greek heathen cultures, people believed in many gods having supernatural powers. The gods are too many to name, representing everything under the sun. The Greeks made images of theirs gods and used these images in worship.

Any organization using a mythological god as its namesake is not based on truth, but on a false god. In 1 Thessalonians 5:22, we are told to "abstain from all appearance of evil." So how can we participate in activities that involve reveling and drinking and feel as if God sanctions these behaviors?

If we bring pictures or objects showing mythological gods into our homes or wear them on our persons, we are inviting demons associated with these gods to enter our bodies or our domain. Any half-human, half-animal symbol is a pagan icon and therefore demonic.

Examples of Mythological Gods

Ulysses – god of bravery.

Endymion – god of fertility and of eternal youth.

Isis – goddess of fertility.

Thoth – Egyptian god of wisdom and science.

Poseidon – god of the sea.

Bacchus – god of wine and inebriation.

Proteus – shepherd god of the oceans.

Argus – Greek god with a thousand eyes.

Zeus – chief ruler of all the Greek gods.

Saturn – Roman god of agriculture, time, and celebration.

Atlas – a titan in Greek mythology who carried the world on his shoulders.

Pandora – the first woman created, according to Greek mythology.

Allah – Muslim god.

Okeanos – Greek god of oceans and fertile valleys.

Rea – mother of Zeus.

Hercules – son of Zeus and legendary strongman of ancient Greece.

Thor – Scandinavian god of rain and thunder.

Pegasus – white-winged horse of Greek gods.

Aphrodite – Greek goddess of love and sex. Romans called her Venus. The Bible called her Ashtoreth, Ishtar, Astarte, or the Queen of Heaven.

Momus – Greek god of mockery and son of night.

Minerva – daughter of Zeus.

Hermes – messenger to the gods. Romans call him Mercury.

Iris – goddess of the rainbow.

Armor – god of eroticism and sensuality. Romans called him Eros or Cupid.

Diana – moon goddess.

Babylon – represents all that is false in religion.

This is not a complete list of ancient heathen gods, but you can see how we Christians have been led astray and into compromise so slowly and gently that we were not aware what was happening to us.

Search for yourself and see what God wants you to do in any given situation. Do not take my word for it. Your eternal destiny is at stake in this life. Time is fleeting and you must by ready for the call of Jesus when He raptures the church home to be ever at His side for eternity.

How to Break Curses

> And the seed of Israel separated themselves from all strangers, and stood and <u>confessed their sins, and the iniquities of their fathers.</u>
>
> —Nehemiah 9:2 KJV (Emphasis mine)

> But if they confess their iniquity and the iniquity of their fathers, with their faithfulness in which they were unfaithful to Me, and that they also have walked contrary to Me, and that I also have walked contrary to them and have brought them into land of their enemies; if their uncircumcised hearts are humbled, and they accept their guilt; then I will remember My covenant with Jacob, and My covenant with Isaac and My covenant with Abraham I will remember; I will remember the land.
>
> —Leviticus 26:40–42 KJV

1. Acknowledge, confess, and repent for your sins and the sins of your ancestors.
2. It is not necessary that you know your ancestors' sins. You can ask God's forgiveness for whatever sins they committed that brought the curse upon your lineage all the way back to Adam and Eve. Ask God to cleanse you, then separate yourself from the sin or sins and whatever displeased God. Place the cross of Calvary and the blood of Jesus between the curse and yourself or your family members.
3. You can then ask God to remove the curse He has allowed upon your life due to the sins that caused the curse to be manifested.

4. Now you can command the demons that have been manifesting the curse in your life to leave you in the name of Jesus.
5. Speak to your body in the name of Jesus and command the manifestations of the curse to leave your body. Speak the Word, quoting healing Scripture passages, and command restoration of your body in the name of Jesus.
6. Cover yourself and your family members with the blood of Jesus, shielding you and them from the demonic spirits that have caused the curse or the curses.

Conclusion

The purpose of this study guide is to ignite in you a zealous passion for the Word of God, to help you know a more peaceful and meaningful walk with the Creator, and to provide you with the tools for a more victorious life.

The divine Word contains the mysteries of the universe, and God is just waiting for you to search its contents for answers to the myriad of questions that lie unanswered in your life.

The Holy Spirit is waiting, gently and patiently wooing you into His presence to join Him in the greatest love affair of all time, which will culminate with eternity. What a spectacular thought— eternity with the King! When you stand before Him, beholding Him in His full glory, all else will fade away! All the trials, pain, uncertainty, rejections, loneliness, temptations, and tears will be gone forever. There will be no looking back, and you can look toward a wonderful future of endless time spent with your glorious and awesome Father God.

Do you want to stand before Him without regrets? I do. The only way to fulfill this desire is to find out everything you can about God and get to know Him intimately. When you begin to know His heart, you start the journey toward becoming just like Him, seeing things as He sees them, wanting the things He wants, responding the way He responds, thinking the way He thinks, hurting when He hurts, and rejoicing when He rejoices.

What an awesome privilege God has given you by allowing you to join Him on this journey from fallen man to transformation into His image!

The decision is all yours. What will you do with this newfound information, this door of knowledge to a walk with the King of the universe?

"Behold, I stand at the door, and knock: if any man hear my voice, and open the door, I will come in to him, and will sup with him, and he with me.

To him that overcometh will I grant to sit with me in my throne, even as I also overcame, and am set down with my Father in his throne.

He that hath an ear, let him hear what the Spirit saith unto the churches." (Revelation 3:20–22 KJV).

Home Study Guide

As you went through this study, did you see any pattern or patterns emerging that have plagued your family perhaps for generations? Ask God to show you any hidden generational curses in your lineage.

- ✗ Is there emotional illness or depression in your family tree that has remained for any length of time?
- ✗ Is there suicide in your family tree?
- ✗ Is there alcoholism in one or both of your parents, your grandparents, or other relatives?
- ✗ Are there drug or other chemical addictions in your relatives?
- ✗ Can you trace any physical illness you might have to other family members past or present? For example is there high blood pressure, diabetes, heart trouble, cancer, or multiple scleroris?
- ✗ Has poverty plagued you or any of your family members? How far back in your lineage does the poverty go?
- ✗ Has any family member past or present verbally, emotionally, physically, or sexually abused another person or persons?
- ✗ Can you trace family members who have had problems controlling their weight?
- ✗ Have family members past or present had anger or rage issues? Do you?
- ✗ Do you or other family members have a perverse spirit? (Sexual sins, which fall under this category, include but are not limited to pornography, adultery, sex before marriage, multiply sexual partners, bestiality, and a lustful spirit.)
- ✗ Did you or any family member become pregnant or father a child outside of marriage?
- ✗ Is divorce a constant in your family?
- ✗ Can you trace homosexuality in any of your family members?

Even if there are no curses in your lineage, and I doubt this is possible, you can start a generational curse in yourself and your children by disobedience to God's commands found in His Word. Sin is always the vehicle that opens the door to generational curses and allows the fiery darts of the Enemy to penetrate our armor, giving Satan the opportunity to "sift us as wheat."

You may think your actions will not affect those around you, but you are mistaken. Go back through the study and see for yourself. Did not the sin of Adam and Eve affect all generations that followed?

As the Holy Spirit illuminates hidden curses in your life, go to the next section, "Prayer for Deliverance," and process these curses in a godly way. It is time to let the past be in the past!

Prayer for Deliverance

Father, I come to You in the name of Jesus, acknowledging not only my sins, but the sins of my ancestors all the way back to Adam and Eve. I ask You to forgive my ancestors as well as me for _____. (Fill in the blank if you know the sin. If not, ask God to forgive whatever sins brought the curse upon you and your family. It is not necessary to know the exact sin.)

I ask You to cleanse me from these iniquities as I separate myself wholly apart for Your service. Father, I place the cross of Calvary and the blood of Jesus between the curse and immediate family members and myself.

I ask You to remove the curse from my life and the lives of my children.

Satan, the Lord Jesus and the blood of Jesus rebuke you and command you and the demons that have been manifesting the curse to leave in the name of Jesus.

I speak to my body, my finances, and my health and call forth the blessing of the Most High. (Speak the Word, quoting the promises of God's Word to your situation.)

I cover my family as well as myself with the precious blood of the Lamb. (Do this daily.)

Notes

Notes

Notes

Notes

Notes

Carolyn Dupuy

Notes

Illustrations

Illustration 1 – Spirit, Soul & Body...1
Illustration 2 – Spiritual Cycle 16
Illustration 3 – Shield of Faith...29

Bibliography

John and Paula Sanford, The Transformation of the Inner Man (Tulsa, OK 74136; Victory House, Inc. 1982)

John and Paula Sanford, Healing the Wounded Spirit (Tulsa, OK 74136; Victory House, Inc. 1985)

Liberty S. Savard, Shattering Your Strongholds (South Plainfield, NJ 07080; Bridge Publishing Inc. 1995)

Rebecca Brown, M.D. and Daniel M. Yoder, Unbroken Curses; (Springdale, PA 15144; Whitaker House 1995)

Larry Huch, Free at Last; (Portland, Oregon 97213; Larry Huch Ministries 2000)

Webster's Collegiate Dictionary, Electronic Edition, 1994, 1995

Encyclopedia Britannica 14th Edition

Dr. Caroline Leaf, Who Switched Off My Brain (Printed in USA by Switch on Your Brain P.O. Box 4227 Riovonia 2128 South Africa)

About the Author

The birth of Recovery Outreach Ministry in 1991 was the result of my own need for healing and wholeness. The process toward recovery and wholeness that God had started in my own life sparked the desire to help others who were experiencing repeated patterns of dysfunctional behavior. Having begun this process, I was anxious to be a part of God's plan to offer them solutions to their pain.

Through guidance from the Holy Spirit, I was led to the Word and to many Christian tapes and books dealing with all types of dysfunctional behavior. Whether this behavior resulted from the abuse of food, sex, alcohol, or mood or mind-altering chemicals or from incest, rape, damaged emotions, or unmet needs, I discovered that the answers were in the Holy Bible. They were there all along just waiting to be discovered so that I could gain freedom and become all that God had called me to be.

"The Lord bless thee, and keep thee: The Lord make his face shine upon thee, and be gracious unto thee: The Lord lift up his countenance upon thee, and give thee peace" (Numbers 6:24–26).